Perfect
Party Games

Stephen Curtis

BOOKS

Published by Random House Books 2010

10 9 8 7 6 5 4 3 2 1

First published in the United Kingdom in 2010 by

Random House Books
Random House, 20 Vauxhall Bridge Road,
London SW1V 2SA

www.rbooks.co.uk

Addresses for companies within The Random House Group Limited can be found at:
www.randomhouse.co.uk/offices.htm

The Random House Group Limited Reg. No. 954009

A CIP catalogue record for this book
is available from the British Library

ISBN 9781847945624

The Random House Group Limited supports The Forest Stewardship
Council (FSC), the leading international forest certification organisation. All our
titles that are printed on Greenpeace approved FSC certified paper carry the FSC logo.
Our paper procurement policy can be found at www.rbooks.co.uk/environment

Mixed Sources

Product group from well-managed
forests and other controlled sources
www.fsc.org Cert no. TT-COC-2139
© 1996 Forest Stewardship Council

Typeset by Palimpsest Book Production Limited, Grangemouth, Stirlingshire
Printed and bound in Great Britain by CPI Bookmarque, Croydon CR0 4TD

Contents

Introduction

The family that plays together . . . often has a jolly good time.

I don't wish to make excessive claims for the beneficial effects of party games, but many people will look back fondly to the games they played as children, supervised or unsupervised. I can remember as a child looking forward to the chance of playing a 'family game' at Christmas. I can remember my own children begging to play similar games. I can also remember parties at which both generations, separately or together, played and really enjoyed the sorts of games listed in this book.

Today's children have opportunities for play that previous generations never had. No one, I think, would want to deprive them of the pleasures of the Wii, the computer or other assorted electronic gadgets. At the same time, perhaps, everyone is slightly relieved when children nowadays show that they realise that play can involve more than pressing buttons with dazzling rapidity. There will, hopefully, always be a place for the kinds of games described in this book. People, hopefully, will always want to organise parties – if only for a change or in order to save a little money – in which fun can be generated from everyday objects such as pencils and paper, balls, beanbags and balloons. If you think you might want to arrange such an event for a group of children, for the family, or even for a group of adults, then this is the book for you.

In choosing games to include here, I have strayed slightly beyond the strict definition of a party game. In addition to games for everyone from small children to adults, and games of every type, from the very traditional such as I WROTE A LETTER TO MY LOVE and ORANGES AND LEMONS, to the very modern, designed for trampolines and parachutes, I have put in a few easy, but often uproarious, card games, and some travel games too. The idea has been to provide a compendium of useful and enjoyable games for a variety of occasions.

In most cases the games are identified by their familiar traditional names. Where the games are not traditional, the names are not necessarily familiar, of course. In some cases, people have described games to me without knowing exactly what they are called. If I have not been able to discover a generally used name, I have had to invent one. I apologise in advance to anyone who discovers a game that they know by one name appearing under another or what appears to be the 'wrong' name. I hope that the name change doesn't detract from the fun of playing the game in question.

How to use this book

The vast majority of games in this book have been described systematically, so that the reader can see at a glance what sort of game is in question, how many can play, what resources you need to play it, etc. Occasionally, games that are fairly similar to other games have been described more cursorily, with a cross reference to the related game where you can find additional information.

The games themselves are listed in alphabetical order beginning with ALL TIED UP and running through to ZIP AND BONG. There is, therefore, no need for an ordinary index. Instead, I have provided an index that lists games by type. If, for instance, you particularly want to find a quiet game or a trampoline game, you can go to the relevant section of the index where games of that type will be listed.

I have also included a couple of additional features that I hope readers will find useful. There is, for instance, a list of forfeits for games where getting it wrong entails paying a small penalty. There are various other lists as well, for example a list of film titles to accompany the game PENS, PAPER, ACTION!. These are anything but definitive, and you yourself will usually be able to come up with better ideas that suit your own guests. Finally, on pp. 196–198, you will find 12 tips for organising a successful party with games and a specimen timetable for a party for children aged 4 to 8. Good luck and good partying!

Acknowledgements

Many people have contributed to the making of this book. I should particularly like to thank Philip Warren, Chery Othen-Lucas, Andrew Hill, Barry and Shirley Jeffery, Shanti, Saskia and Lewis Bahadur and Tom Curtis for directly or indirectly adding to the contents. From the outset, however, I have relied on my wife, Sally, a former infants and junior teacher of vast experience, for expert guidance and active help in researching the material. Without her, the book could not have been written.

All tied up

TYPE OF GAME: A team game that tests dexterity
WHO CAN PLAY: Children and adults
HOW MANY CAN PLAY: The game works best with 8–12 players
WHERE YOU PLAY: Indoors

What you need

Two longish pieces of string, each with a variety of different items tied on to it (there should be one item for each team member). Possibilities include: plastic cups, kitchen utensils, scarves, socks, balloons, etc. (anything can be used that fits the purpose)

How you play

Divide the players into two equal teams. The teams sit in lines facing each other. The person at the head of each line is given a piece of string with items attached. On the word 'Go!', they both start untying one item from the string. When they have finished, they pass on the string to the next member of their team.

Aim of the game

To be the first team with an empty string

Vital rules

The items on the two strings should be the same or similar to ensure fairness

Alphabet tales

TYPE OF GAME: A travel word game
WHO CAN PLAY: Older children and adults
HOW MANY CAN PLAY: Up to 6 players
WHERE YOU PLAY: In a car or on the train

What you need

No resources required

How you play

This is an alphabet game that tells a story. The first player thinks of a sentence beginning with the letter 'A', for example 'A was an apple'. The second player continues the story: 'B bought it'; then 'C collected it'; then 'D drew it' and so on through the letters of the alphabet. Each incident must be related to the one that went before.

Aim of the game

To tell a story from player to player going right through the alphabet

Vital rules

A player who fails to invent part of the story in the five seconds given has to drop out. If nobody has won by the time you get to 'Z', the game begins again

Angels and devils

TYPE OF GAME: A travel game
WHO CAN PLAY: Older children and adults
HOW MANY CAN PLAY: Up to 7 players
WHERE YOU PLAY: In the car

What you need

No resources required

How you play

Passengers in the car are divided into teams: Angels and Devils. As a car passes, the numbers on the plates are added up. If the numbers total less than 13, that is a point to the Angels. Over 13 and the Devils take the point.

Aim of the game

To score the most points

Vital rules

If the numbers add up to exactly 13 then the point goes to whichever side shouts out its team name first

NOTE: The new numbering system for vehicle registration plates, introduced in the UK in 2001, may give an overwhelming advantage to the Angels. As of the end of 2009, the highest value for a new-style number plate was 14 (59). As there are still plenty of pre-2001 vehicles on the road, it may be possible to play the game according to the original rules. It may equally be possible to play to those rules when driving abroad. Parents/organisers should be prepared to set a new boundary number (say ten) to distinguish Angels from Devils if necessary.

Animal, vegetable or mineral

TYPE OF GAME: A guessing game
WHO CAN PLAY: Older children and adults
HOW MANY CAN PLAY: Any number
WHERE YOU PLAY: Indoors

What you need

No resources required

How you play

One player thinks of a person, place or thing and tells the other players whether it is animal (any kind of living and moving being), vegetable (any kind of plant or anything made from plant materials such as wood) or mineral (rocks, stones, objects made of metal, etc.). The other players are allowed 20 questions to find out what it is. The answers to those questions are restricted to 'Yes', 'No', 'Partly' or 'Sometimes'. The player who discovers the answer is the winner.

Aim of the game

To discover the person, place or thing that is in the player's mind by asking questions

Aunt Dee is dead

TYPE OF GAME: A copycat game
WHO CAN PLAY: Children and adults
HOW MANY CAN PLAY: Any number
WHERE YOU PLAY: Indoors

What you need

No resources required

How you play

The players sit round in a circle. The first player turns to the player on his or her left and says 'Did you know that Aunt Dee is dead?' The second player answers 'How did she die?' The first player replies with something like 'She died with one eye closed.' He or she then closes one eye and keeps it closed for the rest of the game. The second player turns to the player on his or her left, goes through the same conversation and then likewise remains with one eye closed. The game continues around the circle until all players have been through the same conversation and closed one eye. The first player then has another turn. Keeping one eye closed as before, he or she adds to the peculiarities, saying perhaps, 'She died with one eye closed and her hand on her heart.' This description is passed around the circle in the same way until all the players have one eye closed and their hand on their heart. The object of the game is to add another peculiarity each time while continuing to hold the others. Anyone who breaks the chain is out. The last one to hold out is the winner.

Aim of the game

To copy and maintain all the actions mentioned by the lead player

Balloon dance

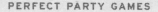

TYPE OF GAME: An active, noisy game
WHO CAN PLAY: Children and adults
HOW MANY CAN PLAY: Any even number, as the game is played
   in couples
WHERE YOU PLAY: Indoors in a large room

What you need

Inflated balloons tied to pieces of string (elastic can be used for a safer game)

How you play

Each player has a balloon tied to one ankle. Partners are chosen and everyone dances, while at the same time trying to burst other couples' balloons by stamping on them. The winners are the last surviving couple with at least one balloon. If a couple lose both their balloons, they are out of the game.

Aim of the game

To keep your own balloon from being burst, while bursting everyone else's

NOTE: This game is apt to become something of a riot so it may be a good idea to appoint a referee to ensure fair play.

Balloon-popping relay

TYPE OF GAME: A team game
WHO CAN PLAY: Older children and adults
HOW MANY CAN PLAY: 8 or more players
WHERE YOU PLAY: In a large indoor space

What you need

Two black bin liners full of inflated balloons (one for each member of the team); two chairs

How you play

Put the two chairs at one end of the room, with the black bags full of inflated balloons beside them. Divide the players into two teams. The teams line up together at the opposite end of the room to the chairs. On the word 'Go!' the first person in each team runs to their team's chair, takes a balloon from the bag, puts it on the chair, and sits on it to pop it. When the balloon has popped, the player runs back to the team and touches the next person, who then repeats the process. The first team to burst all the balloons in its bag is the winner.

Aim of the game

To burst all the balloons in your team's bag

Balloon race

TYPE OF GAME: A fairly active indoor racing game
WHO CAN PLAY: Children and active adults
HOW MANY CAN PLAY: 6–8 players depending on space
WHERE YOU PLAY: A large room with the furniture pushed back

What you need

A round balloon and cardboard tube or rolled-up piece of paper for each player; something to mark the start and the finishing line

How you play

The game is a race (with a proper start and a finishing line) in which each player uses the tube to blow his or her balloon to the other end of the room.

Aim of the game

To be the first to blow your balloon to the finishing line

Vital rules

If your balloon touches the floor you must start again

Variations

DARTING FISH (p. 40)

Banana relay

TYPE OF GAME: A sitting-down musical game
WHO CAN PLAY: People of any age
HOW MANY CAN PLAY: 6 players minimum, but the more the better
WHERE YOU PLAY: Indoors

What you need

A banana; a CD player or other music source

How you play

One player is chosen to be the 'guesser' and stands in the middle of a circle made by the others. One of the players in the circle has a banana, which is passed along behind the players' backs while the music plays. The banana can be passed in either direction and players can change the direction in which it is being passed at any time. The aim of the players in the circle is to fool the guesser. So, one or other of them may decide to keep hold of the banana and simply pretend to pass it on. When this happens, other players must continue the pretence, passing an imaginary banana in one direction or the other. When the music stops, the guesser must guess who has the banana. If the guesser gets it right, he or she changes places with the person holding the banana. If not, he or she must guess again. (Generally, the guesser is allowed back into the circle after three wrong guesses.)

Aim of the game

To guess which of the players in the circle is holding the banana, or to fool the guesser

Variations

HUNT THE SLIPPER (p. 75)

Bang bang relay

TYPE OF GAME: A lively racing game
WHO CAN PLAY: Children and active adults
HOW MANY CAN PLAY: 8–16 players
WHERE YOU PLAY: Indoors

What you need

A chair for each player; one paper bag for each player and spares for demonstrating

How you play

Arrange the chairs in two rows, facing one another about 2 metres apart, and place a paper bag on each chair. Then divide the players into two teams. Each player sits on a bag on a chair. On 'Go!' the two players at the top of the rows run round the back of their teams, up the middle, and back to their chairs where they must blow up a bag and burst it by sitting on it. The bang is the signal for the next team member to run to the end of the row, behind the team, up the middle, and back to his or her chair to burst the bag. The first team to burst all its bags is the winner.

Aim of the game

To burst all your team's bags

Vital rules

The next player cannot proceed until the bag has been burst

Variations

Party poppers could be used instead of paper bags

Beetle

TYPE OF GAME: A popular sitting-down family game
WHO CAN PLAY: Children and adults
HOW MANY CAN PLAY: Usually up to 8 players
WHERE YOU PLAY: Indoors at a table

What you need

A dice; paper and a pencil for each player

How you play

The aim is to draw a beetle with a body, head, tail, legs, feelers and eyes. The numbers on the dice correspond to different parts of the beetle: 6 = the body; 5 = the head; 4 = the tail; 3 = a leg; 2 = a feeler, 1 = an eye. A full beetle has one body, one head, one tail, six legs, two eyes and two feelers. The parts must be drawn in a logical order. You must start with a body (you cannot draw a head, legs, tail, etc., until you have thrown a six to get a body). Likewise you cannot add eyes and feelers until you have a head.

Aim of the game

To be the first to draw a complete beetle

NOTE: The organiser should draw a demonstration beetle for the benefit of those playing for the first time.

Variations

There are manufactured versions of this game, but it can also work very well when original beetles are drawn. There are also alternative ways of numbering the parts of the beetle's body (for example, 1 = body;

2 = head; 3 = legs; 4 = eyes; 5 = feelers; 6 = tail). It can sometimes take a very long time to throw six threes to get six legs, so variations can be introduced into the rules to cope with this (for example, 3 = a pair of legs)

Black magic

TYPE OF GAME: A guess-the-trick game
WHO CAN PLAY: Children and adults
HOW MANY CAN PLAY: Any number
WHERE YOU PLAY: Indoors

What you need

No resources required

How you play

Two players (organiser and accomplice) need to know the trick. The organiser asks for a volunteer to do some black magic, selects the accomplice and sends him or her out of the room. The organiser asks the remaining players to select any item in the room that is on view. Once they have made their selection, the accomplice is called in and told that he or she must discover by magic which item has been selected. The organiser points to various items in the room that are not coloured black, asking 'Is it this?' or 'Is it that?' The answer is 'No'. After a few exchanges of this kind, the organiser points to something that is black and asks 'Is it this?' This question is a signal to the accomplice, who then knows that the next item asked about will be the one that was chosen. The game continues until everyone has guessed the trick.

Aim of the game

To guess the trick

Blind man's buff

TYPE OF GAME: An active guessing game – a very old and very popular parlour game

WHO CAN PLAY: Fit players of any age

HOW MANY CAN PLAY: It depends on the amount of space available

WHERE YOU PLAY: Indoors or outdoors. Wherever you play, there should be a fair amount of clear space

What you need

A blindfold

How you play

The player chosen to start the game is blindfolded and turned around or asked to turn around. He or she then sets out to catch the other players, who try to dodge out of the way. When the blindfolded player makes a catch, he or she has to guess the identity of the person caught before raising the blindfold. If this is done successfully, the players change places and the game starts again.

Aim of the game

To catch and identify another player

Variations

A traditional way of starting the chase is for the other players to ask the blindfolded player the question 'How many horses has your father got?' When the blindfolded player answers 'three', the others ask 'What colour are they?' The chaser answers 'black, white and grey'. Then the rest call out 'Turn around three times and catch who you may.'

The chaser turns around three times and then tries to catch someone. These questions and answers are very old and could easily be adapted to a more modern chant, or indeed left out altogether

See also BLIND MAN'S STICK (below); SQUEAK, PIGGY, SQUEAK (p. 166); WHO'S PIG? (p. 192)

Blind man's stick

TYPE OF GAME: A fairly active guessing game
WHO CAN PLAY: Children and adults
HOW MANY CAN PLAY: The game needs more than 6 players to work well
WHERE YOU PLAY: Usually indoors. Push furniture back to provide adequate space

What you need

A blindfold; some kind of stick

How you play

The players form a circle. One person is blindfolded and stands in the centre holding a stick. The circle must keep moving round. The person in the centre keeps the stick low and with it gently touches one person in the circle. The player who has been touched takes hold of the stick and the circle stops moving. The blindfolded player now imitates an animal noise or someone saying a familiar catchphrase (such as 'Nice to see you, to see you nice!', 'Because you're worth it', 'Evening all'). The person holding the other end of the stick must copy the noise or catchphrase. The blindfolded player then has to guess who it is. If he or she is successful, the person holding the other end of the stick is blindfolded and goes into the middle.

Aim of the game

To guess who is holding the other end of the stick

Vital rules

The stick must be held low to avoid injury

Variations

BLIND MAN'S BUFF (p. 13); SQUEAK, PIGGY, SQUEAK (p. 166); WHO'S PIG? (p. 192)

Bounce once more

TYPE OF GAME: A trampoline game
WHO CAN PLAY: Children
HOW MANY CAN PLAY: 2 players at a time
WHERE YOU PLAY: Outdoors, or in a large indoor space

What you need

A trampoline

How you play

Each player starts by doing a single seat-drop (sit-down) and a bounce. Then two seat-drops and a bounce, then three seat-drops and a bounce, and so on. The first player to get to ten seat-drops is the winner. If there are more than two players, the others can be watching and counting while waiting for their go.

Aim of the game

To be the first to do ten seat-drops and a bounce

Bounce the Buddha

> **TYPE OF GAME:** A trampoline game
> **WHO CAN PLAY:** Children
> **HOW MANY CAN PLAY:** Up to 5 children, depending on the size of the trampoline
> **WHERE YOU PLAY:** Outdoors, or in a large indoor space

What you need

A trampoline

How you play

One child is chosen to be the Buddha. The chosen child sits in the middle of the trampoline with legs crossed and arms folded, elbows pointing outwards as if in meditation. The others bounce around the Buddha trying to get him to wobble and fall over. The Buddha must keep his arms folded. The Buddha changes places with another player when he topples over.

Aim of the game

For the Buddha: to stay in position; for the other players: to make the Buddha topple over

Bouncing balls

What you need

A parachute; two or three foam footballs

How you play

The children stand round the parachute holding the handles at chest height. Two children are chosen to be underneath it. The three balls are thrown into the centre of the parachute. The children underneath must try to knock the balls off the parachute, while the children holding the handles must try to keep them on.

Aim of the game

For the children underneath: to knock the balls off the parachute; for the children around the edge: to keep the balls on the parachute

Bouncing bullets

> **TYPE OF GAME:** A parachute game
> **WHO CAN PLAY:** Children
> **HOW MANY CAN PLAY:** It depends on the size of the parachute
> **WHERE YOU PLAY:** Outdoors, or in a large indoor space

What you need

A parachute; around 12 plastic balls, half of one colour and half of another

How you play

The children stand round the parachute. The players on one side of the parachute become one team, and take all the balls of one colour. Those on the other side become the other team, taking the balls of the other colour. The children make large waves and the balls are thrown into the middle, flying about in all directions. The team that bounces all its balls off the parachute first wins the game.

Aim of the game

To bounce all your team's balls off the parachute

Variations

This game can be played with one large soft ball or a soft toy. Each team must try to send it flying off on the opposing team's side to win a point

Bridge the word

What you need

Paper and pencils

How you play

Draw six straight lines one below the other across a piece of paper. Choose a six-letter word. Starting at the top, write the letters of the chosen word in order at the left-hand ends of the lines you have drawn. Then, starting at the bottom, write the letters again, in order at the right-hand ends of the lines. If the word you chose was, for example, 'person', you would have a grid looking like this:

```
P_____N
E_____O
R_____S
S_____R
O_____E
N_____P
```

Players now take it in turns to think of a word that will 'bridge' those letters, i.e. begin with a 'P' and end with an 'N', begin with an 'E' and end with an 'O', etc. The player who thinks of the longest word wins.

Aim of the game

To think of the longest word you know that has the first and last letters you have been given

Bring me

TYPE OF GAME: A team searching game
WHO CAN PLAY: Children and adults
HOW MANY CAN PLAY: Two teams of 6–8 players
WHERE YOU PLAY: Indoors

What you need

A list of everyday items easily found inside a home and/or things likely to be found on the players, for example a lady's watch, a gentleman's handkerchief, a necklace, a coin of a particular value

How you play

The players are divided into two teams. The teams sit facing each other at either end of the room. The organiser of the game sits in the middle of the room and reads out the first item on the list. The first team to find the item and place it in the organiser's hand scores a point. It adds to the fun if the items can only be delivered by the youngest member of the team, particularly if young children wish to be involved.

Aim of the game

To score the most points

Vital rules

An uneven number of items on the list will ensure that one team wins

British bulldog

TYPE OF GAME: A traditional chasing game
WHO CAN PLAY: Children
HOW MANY CAN PLAY: Any number
WHERE YOU PLAY: Outdoors, in a large playing area with 2
    distinct ends

What you need

No resources required

How you play

One person is chosen to be the 'bulldog' and stands in the middle of
the play area. All the other players wait together at one end of the area.
When the bulldog shouts 'Go!', they must run to the other end without
being tagged by the bulldog. If a player is tagged, he or she becomes
an extra bulldog and remains in the middle to help tag on the next go.
The number of bulldogs increases until, at last, only one player remains
– the winner.

Aim of the game

To avoid being tagged by the bulldog

Build a story

What you need

Paper and a pencil for each player

How you play

All the players write down the beginning of a story in four lines and then fold their paper over so that only the last line shows. They then pass their papers to the next player and everyone adds another four lines to the story now in their possession. The story continues around the players in this way until it gets back to the writer of the first four lines, who then writes the ending. The stories are then read aloud.

Aim of the game

To make up amusing stories

Build a word

What you need

Paper and a pencil for each player

How you play

Each player in turn reads out the letters on a passing number plate. If the letters make a three-letter word, the player writes it down and scores five points. He or she then looks out for another three letters that will change the word into a six-letter one. For example, having spotted 'HAT' the player may see 'TER', which can be added on to the end to make 'HATTER'. This scores 10 points. If the player spots two actual words that can be put together, for example 'BID' and then later 'DEN', which make 'BIDDEN', he or she scores 15 points. At the end of the game or journey points are added up to decide the winner.

Aim of the game

To score the most points

Button, button

TYPE OF GAME: A quiet guessing game
WHO CAN PLAY: Children and adults
HOW MANY CAN PLAY: Works best with about 10 players
WHERE YOU PLAY: Indoors

What you need

A medium-size button

How you play

All the players sit in a circle with their hands placed palm to palm (as if they were praying) in their laps. One player is given the button, holding it between his or her fingers or palms. The player with the button then goes around the circle to each player in turn, slipping his or her hands between the palms of the other players. The button-holder leaves the button in another player's hands, but continues around the circle for some time, pretending to deposit the button so that the other players do not know who has it. The button-holder then asks 'Who has the button?', and the others have to guess who has it. The player who guesses correctly has the next turn as button-holder.

Aim of the game

To discover who has been given the button

Variations

RING ON A STRING (p. 149)

Buzz

> TYPE OF GAME: A counting and memory game
> WHO CAN PLAY: Older children and adults
> HOW MANY CAN PLAY: Any number
> WHERE YOU PLAY: Indoors

What you need

No resources required

How you play

All the players sit in a circle and begin to count in turn, but whenever someone reaches seven, a number containing seven (e.g. 17, 27), or any multiple of seven (e.g. 14, 21, 28, 35) they must say 'buzz' in its place. For example, in the forties, the count should go: '40, 41, buzz, 43, 44, 45, 46, buzz, 48, buzz, 50.' In the seventies, players should use the form 'buzz one, buzz two, buzz three', and so on. When anyone forgets to say 'buzz' or says it in the wrong place, he or she is out. When someone is out, the count can go back to one, but it is usually more fun if the players continue on, as things get more fraught when the count is up in the hundreds. The game continues as long as is desired.

Aim of the game

To keep the game going until you reach a really high number by not forgetting to say 'buzz'

Variations

Numbers other than seven can be used

Cat and mouse

TYPE OF GAME: An energetic chasing game
WHO CAN PLAY: Children of any age
HOW MANY CAN PLAY: Any number
WHERE YOU PLAY: Indoors or outdoors, in a large open space

What you need

No resources required

How you play

The players form a circle in the centre of the area. They hold hands and stretch out their arms. The 'mouse' is chosen and creeps round outside the circle, then taps the back of one of the children in the ring. The tapped child becomes the cat. The cat now chases the mouse in and out of the ring until the mouse is caught. The mouse then rejoins the ring, and the child who played the cat becomes the mouse. The game starts again.

Aim of the game

To catch the mouse

Variations

I WROTE A LETTER TO MY LOVE (p. 84); RACE ME ROUND (p. 147)

Cat and mouse (parachute)

> TYPE OF GAME: A parachute game
> WHO CAN PLAY: Children aged 3 and over
> HOW MANY CAN PLAY: It depends on the size of the parachute
> WHERE YOU PLAY: Outdoors, or in a large indoor space

What you need

A parachute

How you play

Two or three children are chosen to be the mice (the number depends on the size of the parachute and how many children are playing). Another child is chosen to be the cat. All the other children sit around the edge of the parachute, holding it up by the handles. The mice are sent under the parachute and the other children make waves. The cat then prowls on top of the parachute looking for the mice. When the cat spots a mouse shape he or she pounces (kneels down beside the shape and puts his or her arms around it). The caught mouse must then come out from underneath and join the others. When all the mice have been caught, the players change over and the game starts again.

Aim of the game

For the cat: to catch the mice; for the mice: to avoid being caught

Catch and count

TYPE OF GAME: A family game
WHO CAN PLAY: Children and adults
HOW MANY CAN PLAY: 6 players
WHERE YOU PLAY: Indoors

What you need

Sets of cut-out cardboard fish with numbers from one to ten written on them (about three fish per player), with a large paper clip on each fish's mouth; six garden canes with a string tied to one end and a large magnet tied to the other end of the string

How you play

The fish are shuffled and placed, numbers down, on the floor. The players stand or sit round a 'pond' and on the word 'Go!' they catch as many fish as possible. At the end of a set time they add up the scores on the fish they have caught. The person with the highest score is the winner.

Aim of the game

To score the most points by catching the highest-value fish

Variations

The game could be played with one 'rod', the players taking it in turns to have a go

Catching the kangaroo

TYPE OF GAME: An active game
WHO CAN PLAY: Anyone who can throw and catch
HOW MANY CAN PLAY: Any number, depending on the space available
WHERE YOU PLAY: Outdoors

What you need

A rubber ball or beanbag

How you play

One player is chosen to be the 'hunter'. All the other players stand in a circle, with the hunter in the middle. The ball or beanbag is the 'kangaroo'. It is passed round and round the circle and sometimes thrown across it. The hunter has to try to catch it. When the hunter succeeds, the player who should have caught the kangaroo goes into the circle instead.

Aim of the game

To catch the kangaroo

Vital rules

The kangaroo must be thrown across the circle as well as passed around from player to player

Variations

A well-known version of this game is 'Piggy in the middle'

Catch the mouse

TYPE OF GAME: A trampoline game
WHO CAN PLAY: Children
HOW MANY CAN PLAY: 2 players
WHERE YOU PLAY: Outdoors, or in a large indoor space

What you need

A trampoline

How you play

One child is the cat and one is the mouse. They both move around the edge of the trampoline, avoiding the 'pond' in the middle. The cat tries to catch the mouse and pull him or her into the centre.

Aim of the game

For the cat to catch the mouse

Change places

TYPE OF GAME: A parachute game
WHO CAN PLAY: Children
HOW MANY CAN PLAY: It depends on the size of the parachute
WHERE YOU PLAY: Outdoors, or a large indoor space

What you need

A parachute

How you play

Children sit around the edge of the parachute holding the handles. The leader calls the names of two children on opposite sides of the parachute and says 'Change places'. The two children must then crawl underneath the parachute and attempt to come out at the right place.

Aim of the game

To give everyone a chance at crawling underneath the parachute

Variations

Tell the children to lift the parachute high overhead to form a mushroom and lower their arms slowly. When the mushroom has formed, call a child's name and tell him or her to crawl, hop, skip or walk, etc., to the other side. The chosen child must then crawl, hop, skip or walk, etc., to the other side before the parachute touches him or her

Charades

TYPE OF GAME: A traditional miming game
WHO CAN PLAY: Older children and adults
HOW MANY CAN PLAY: Any number
WHERE YOU PLAY: Indoors

What you need

No resources required

How you play

The players sit in a circle. The organiser writes down the name of a film, book or play and passes it to one of the players (see p. 204 for some suggestions for titles). This player must step into the circle and mime the title for everyone to guess.

There are certain conventions in this game. When you are doing a mime, you should first indicate whether the title you are miming belongs to a film, book or play. To indicate a film, hold one hand still and make a movement with the other as if you are turning a handle rapidly; to indicate a book, put your two hands together with the palms touching, then open them up; to indicate a play, move your hands as if they were the curtains opening in a theatre.

It is usual to mime the words in the title syllable by syllable. Tap one finger on your arm to show that you are miming the first syllable, two fingers for the second syllable, and so on. Sometimes it is easier to mime a word or syllable that 'sounds like' the word or syllable you actually want (for instance if you had to mime 'Kwai' in *Bridge on the River Kwai*). Touch your ear to indicate 'sounds like'. To indicate a 'short word', such as 'the', hold your thumb and forefinger a short distance apart (the other players can often fill in short words unaided). To indicate that you are miming the whole word or phrase, draw a circle in the air.

Aim of the game

To mime your title cleverly so that the other players have fun guessing it. It is best if the other players have to make an effort and co-operate with one another to find the answer, but don't make it so difficult that they have to give up

Vital rules

You must not speak at all while doing the mime

Variations

TEAM CHARADES (p. 175)

Chinese whispers

TYPE OF GAME: A listening game
WHO CAN PLAY: Children and adults
HOW MANY CAN PLAY: At least 10 players are needed to make the game work well
WHERE YOU PLAY: Indoors

What you need

No resources required

How you play

The players sit in a line or a circle. The person at the beginning of the line (or at a particular point in the circle) thinks of a statement and whispers it once – just once – to the person sitting next to him or her. That person whispers what he or she thinks the message was to the next person, and so it continues down the line. The last person announces to everyone what he or she had heard. The difference between the first and last message can be amazing.

Aim of the game

To pass the message down the line or around the circle without making any mistakes

Vital rules

The whisper should be loud enough for the next player only to hear

Coming or going

TYPE OF GAME: A fairly quiet team racing game
WHO CAN PLAY: Children and adults
HOW MANY CAN PLAY: At least 12 players
WHERE YOU PLAY: Indoors

What you need

Four large bowls: two empty and two filled with a large number of fairly small but unusual objects (try to make the objects amusing and/or hard to handle)

How you play

The players form two teams and stand side by side in rows facing each other, about 2 metres apart. The two leaders each have a large bowl of objects in front of them and a large empty bowl behind them. On the signal 'Go!', each team leader picks up an object from the bowl and passes it to the next player. As soon as the object has been passed, the team leader picks up another object and passes it on as well. When an object reaches the last person in the row, it is passed around his or her body and returned back along the row behind the player's backs. So at one stage of the game there will be objects being passed one way in front and the other way behind. When the objects arrive back at the beginning of the row, the team leader must place them in the empty bowl behind him or her. The first team to empty the bowl in front and fill the bowl behind wins.

Aim of the game

To be the first team to transfer all your objects from one bowl to the other

Variations

If enough chairs are available, this game can be played sitting down

Confessions

> **TYPE OF GAME:** A sitting-down game
> **WHO CAN PLAY:** Older children and adults
> **HOW MANY CAN PLAY:** Players sit around a large table. The size of the table limits the number of players
> **WHERE YOU PLAY:** Indoors

What you need

Paper and a pencil for each player

How you play

The players sit round the table with a pencil and paper each. The organiser of the game, or 'High Priest', tells everyone to write their name at the top of the paper and fold the paper over two or three times so that the name is well hidden. The High Priest next commands the players to pass the papers round the circle several times to the right, and then back to the left, until nobody knows where the papers originally came from. The High Priest then commands everyone to write down the worst thing they have ever done. This is written underneath the folded portion. For a second time the papers are folded and passed back and forth. When the papers are halted again, the players are commanded to write down 'Why I did it'. The papers are folded and passed on for a third time. When the High Priest finally calls a halt, players unfold the paper in their possession and, in turn, read out the confession.

Aim of the game

To create humorous scenarios

Variations

CONSEQUENCES (p. 36)

Confusions

> TYPE OF GAME: A word game
> WHO CAN PLAY: Adults
> HOW MANY CAN PLAY: Any number
> WHERE YOU PLAY: Indoors

What you need

Pencil and paper for each player

How you play

Each player thinks of the name of an animal, and uses the letters in the name to make other words. For instance, if someone chooses 'elephant', the words might be 'pent heal'; 'monkey' could give 'o my ken'; while 'mackerel' would make 'mere lack'. Allow five minutes for players to make up the anagrams. Each player in turn then reads out his or her 'confusion' to the others, who have to guess what the original word was. Each puzzle is carefully timed and the puzzle that takes the longest to work out is the winner.

Aim of the game

To make a up a clever 'confusion' that will take the other players a long time to unravel

Vital rules

You must use all the letters in the original word (and no others) and you may not use any of them twice. Your confusion must consist of real words

Variations

An easier form of this game is to divide into two teams. Every player chooses a word as above but merely jumbles the letters, so that 'elephant' could become 'phelthane'. The jumbled words are collected and the teams exchange papers. The first team to decode all of the other team's words wins the game or the point

Consequences

TYPE OF GAME: A pencil and paper game
WHO CAN PLAY: Older children and adults
HOW MANY CAN PLAY: It works best with about 8 players
WHERE YOU PLAY: Indoors

What you need

Paper and a pencil for each player

How you play

Each player has a paper and pencil. The players write an adjective that applies to a man at the top of their paper. They fold the top of the paper over and pass it to the right. The players then write the name of a man. They fold the paper over again, and pass it to the right.

Players then add words or phrases in the following order: an adjective applicable to a woman; a woman's name; where they met; what he said to her; what she said to him; the consequence was; and people/the newspapers said . . .

After each addition the paper is folded down and passed to the right. After the final phrase the papers are passed to the right one last time, then opened up and read aloud.

Aim of the game

To create amusing scenarios

Variations

PROGRESSIVE PICTURES (p. 142); MODERN CONSEQUENCES (p. 98)

Court is sitting

TYPE OF GAME: An energetic game
WHO CAN PLAY: Older children familiar with cards, and adults
HOW MANY CAN PLAY: 16 players
WHERE YOU PLAY: Indoors

What you need

Four chairs and a pack of cards

How you play

Put a chair in each corner of the room. The players stand side by side in fours between the chairs, making a square. The aces, kings, queens and jacks of the four suits are shuffled and placed face down in the middle of the square. At a given signal the players each pick up a card. The players who pick up the aces must each get to a chair and declare their suit. The other players must find the ace of the same suit as the card they are holding and they must get themselves into the right order: ace on the chair, king sitting on the ace, queen on the king, jack on the queen. The first four players to arrange themselves correctly are the winners.

Aim of the game

To have all the members of a suit sitting in the correct order on the same chair

Vital rules

Use strong chairs! Players need to be able to take the weight of the others, so children and adults will not usually play together

Variations

This could be played with 12 players if the jacks are removed from the game

Cracked egg

TYPE OF GAME: A trampoline game
WHO CAN PLAY: Older children
HOW MANY CAN PLAY: Up to 6 players
WHERE YOU PLAY: Outdoors, or in a large indoor space

What you need

A trampoline

How you play

One player is chosen to be the 'egg'. The egg sits in the middle of the trampoline, knees bent and hands holding feet. At a given signal the other players bounce up and down, trying to make the egg roll over and 'crack'. If the player who is the egg lets go of his or her feet, or sticks out a leg to retain balance, the egg is cracked and another player takes a turn.

Aim of the game

To crack the egg

Cut cards

TYPE OF GAME: A finding and matching game
WHO CAN PLAY: Children and adults
HOW MANY CAN PLAY: As many as you have space and
    materials for, but it is probably best with 6–8 players
WHERE YOU PLAY: On a large table or on the floor

What you need

A considerable number of old Christmas or birthday cards, or picture postcards

How you play

Cut the cards you are using in half. Scatter the pieces over the top of a table or over the floor. The object of the game is to find as many matching halves as possible, with the person who gets the most being the winner.

Aim of the game

To collect the most matching pairs

Vital rules

This game can get lively. Players should be penalised for pushing or snatching pieces from other players. Perhaps a forfeit (see p. 199) would be in order – or instant disqualification

Variations

MIX AND MATCH (p. 97)

Darting fish

TYPE OF GAME: A boisterous racing game
WHO CAN PLAY: Children aged 4 and above
HOW MANY CAN PLAY: No more than 3 at a time; the game can be played in teams
WHERE YOU PLAY: Indoors

What you need

Some magazines; a selection of paper fish of about 25 cm x 13 cm (10 inches x 5 inches). These can be made from any paper, and decorated (young children would enjoy preparing these in advance)

How you play

Agree a finishing line at one end of the room. At the other end of the room line up the fish, one for each child, then ask the children to kneel behind them. Each child is given a magazine to use as a fan to waft his or her fish along the floor. (Allow the children to practise before the race takes place.) On the word 'Go!' the children must fan their fish to the finishing line. First across is the winner.

Aim of the game

To fan your fish over the finishing line first

Vital rules

Players must not touch the fish or prod it with the magazine

Variations

Divide the players into two teams, so only two fish are required. Each player fans the fish to the finishing line then runs back with it and gives it to the second player, who does the same. The first team whose members have all completed the course wins

Dead lions

TYPE OF GAME: A quiet game, good for calming children down at the end of a party
WHO CAN PLAY: Young children particularly enjoy this game
HOW MANY CAN PLAY: Any number
WHERE YOU PLAY: Indoors or outdoors, but the game involves lying down

What you need

No resources required

How you play

The children all lie quietly, on their backs, on the floor. The adult organiser watches carefully and calls out the name of any child who moves. That child is then out of the game and has to sit at the side. The last person left for 'dead' is the winner.

Aim of the game

To remain very still so that you are not caught out

Do as I do

TYPE OF GAME: A trampoline game
WHO CAN PLAY: Children
HOW MANY CAN PLAY: 2–4 players, depending on the size of the trampoline
WHERE YOU PLAY: Outdoors, or in a large indoor space

What you need

A trampoline

How you play

One child is chosen for the leader. The other children have to copy the leader's movements, keeping their bounces together. Those who fail to follow are out of the game.

Aim of the game

To copy the leader's actions

Dodge ball

TYPE OF GAME: A trampoline game
WHO CAN PLAY: Older children
HOW MANY CAN PLAY: Up to 6 players, depending on the size of the trampoline
WHERE YOU PLAY: Outdoors, or in a large indoor space

What you need

A trampoline; a sponge football

How you play

The football is placed in the middle of the trampoline. The players crouch around it with one finger placed on the ball. They count down 'Three, two, one, go!' On the word 'Go!', they all leave the ball and start to bounce. Each player has two lives. Players who are touched by the ball lose a life and must sit down until another player 'frees' them by touching them. They can then join in again. A player who loses two lives must leave the trampoline. The last one bouncing alongside the ball is the winner.

Aim of the game

To avoid being touched by the ball

Donkey

TYPE OF GAME: A ball game
WHO CAN PLAY: Children enjoy playing this game with adults
HOW MANY CAN PLAY: Any number
WHERE YOU PLAY: Outdoors

What you need

A good ball for catching

How you play

The players stand in a circle and the ball is thrown randomly from player to player. The thrower must call out the name of the person to whom the ball is thrown, to avoid confusion. Players who miss a catch must put their left hand behind their back and catch with their right hand. They become a 'D'. If they miss again, they put their right hand behind their back and catch with their left. They are now an 'O'. On their third miss, players must go down on one knee but may use both hands again, becoming an 'N'. If they miss again, they go down on two knees and become a 'K'. On a fifth miss players must kneel on both knees and put their left hand behind their back. They must now catch only with their right hand and have become an 'E'. When they miss for a sixth time, they put their right hand behind them, catch with their left and become a 'Y'. The next time they miss everyone shouts 'DONKEY!' and that player is out of the game.

Aim of the game

To be the last one left in the game

Vital rules

Unfair throws should not be counted

Double tag

> **TYPE OF GAME:** A chasing and catching game
> **WHO CAN PLAY:** Children
> **HOW MANY CAN PLAY:** Any number
> **WHERE YOU PLAY:** Outdoors, or in a large indoor space

What you need

No resources required

How you play

The children stand in pairs, one behind another, with the pairs forming a circle and everyone facing the centre. One pair of children is chosen to be out of the circle: one child from the pair is to be the 'runner', and the other the 'chaser'. The chaser chases the runner around the outside of the circle, but the runner may dart in and stand in front of any pair for safety and cannot then be tagged. The child at the back of this new line of three then becomes the runner. A runner who is caught before he or she can stand in front of another pair becomes the chaser, and the chaser becomes a runner.

Aim of the game

To avoid being caught

Dressing-up relay

TYPE OF GAME: A racing game
WHO CAN PLAY: Children, but it can be played by adults
HOW MANY CAN PLAY: Enough players to form two teams
WHERE YOU PLAY: Indoors, in a large room

What you need

Two washing-up bowls and two identical sets of clothes – hat, scarf, socks, gloves, etc. (one item for each member of the team); a start line

How you play

The players are divided into two teams. The teams wait at the start line, with the bowls full of clothes at the other end of the room a few feet apart. The first member of each team runs to the bowl, puts on an item of clothing, returns to the start line and gives the item to the next team member, who puts it on, runs to the bowl, puts on a second item of clothing, then wears both items back to his or her team. The second member gives the two items to the third member, who wears them to the bowl, collects yet another item, and so on. The first team to have a fully dressed player back at the start line wins the race.

Aim of the game

To have your last team member back at the start line wearing all the clothes from your team's bowl

Vital rules

The bowls should contain identical sets of clothes if possible

Ducking for apples

TYPE OF GAME: A traditional Halloween game

WHO CAN PLAY: Older children and fun-loving adults

HOW MANY CAN PLAY: From 2 players upwards as turns may be taken

WHERE YOU PLAY: Somewhere where it does not matter if water is spilt

What you need

A large tub or bowl of water with three or four eating apples floating on the top (the number of apples depends on the size of your tub or bowl and the room available around it)

How you play

The players, in turn, or two or three at a time, attempt to grab hold of an apple with their teeth – hands should be held behind the player's back.

Aim of the game

To remove the apples from the water

Vital rules

Hands must not be used

Variations

SWINGING THE APPLE (p. 172)

Easter egg hunt

TYPE OF GAME: A seeking game that requires space
WHO CAN PLAY: Children and chocoholics
HOW MANY CAN PLAY: As many as you have Easter eggs for.
Each player should end up with at least one egg
WHERE YOU PLAY: Indoors and/or outdoors

What you need

Easter eggs – generally, small or tiny eggs are used

How you play

While the players are not around, or before they arrive at the party, the organiser hides a number of Easter eggs in all sorts of places. At the appropriate moment, the players are sent off to find all the eggs. This can be played competitively, with the player who collects the most eggs winning the game. However, it is usually played just for the fun of finding the eggs.

Aim of the game

To find the hidden Easter eggs

Variations

HOW MANY BEANS? (p. 73); ONE FOR TEN (p. 115)

Egg and spoon race

TYPE OF GAME: A traditional racing game
WHO CAN PLAY: Older children
HOW MANY CAN PLAY: Any number
WHERE YOU PLAY: Outdoors

What you need

A dessertspoon and a hard-boiled egg for each player; a start and a finishing line

How you play

The players line up at the start with their egg and spoon on the ground in front of them. On the word 'Go!', the players pick them up and race to the finishing line. They must not touch the egg directly and if it falls off they must stop until they can get it back on their spoon. The first to the finish wins.

Aim of the game

To cross the finishing line first with the egg still on the spoon

Vital rules

The egg must not be handled or held during the race

Variations

Golf balls or potatoes could be used

Feed the baby

What you need

A blindfold (usually improvised from a scarf or handkerchief); a tray of foods for the players to taste – these could include cheese, sugar, custard powder, ginger beer, grated carrot, etc. (try to include some unusual tastes); a tasting spoon for each player

How you play

Each player is given a taste of each food on a spoon, by the organiser. He or she has to guess what it is, and a point is given for every right answer. They then watch the next player go through the 'feeding process'.

Aim of the game

To correctly identify the different foods you taste

Vital rules

No really unpleasant tastes should be offered (and all players must be asked if they have any allergies). Players must not be allowed to see the foods before they taste them. A clean spoon is needed for each player

Variations

This game could be played using various smells or sounds

Filling the gap

> **TYPE OF GAME:** A simple running game
> **WHO CAN PLAY:** Young children particularly enjoy this game,
>   but it can be played by children of any age
> **HOW MANY CAN PLAY:** As many players as the space allows
> **WHERE YOU PLAY:** In a large room or outdoors

What you need

No resources required

How you play

All the players except one make a ring and join hands. A gap is left in
the ring for the additional player. The player walks around outside the
circle and touches someone. Immediately, the first player runs around
the circle in the same direction that he or she had previously been going
to try to 'fill the gap'. The one who has been touched runs in the
opposite direction and tries to fill the gap first. The player who fails to
get into the ring is the one to walk around the next time.

Aim of the game

To beat the other player back to the starting point and 'fill the gap'

Variations

I WROTE A LETTER TO MY LOVE (p. 84)

Find it

TYPE OF GAME: A searching and listening game
WHO CAN PLAY: Children and adults
HOW MANY CAN PLAY: Any number
WHERE YOU PLAY: Indoors

What you need

Any reasonably small but distinctive object that you can hide

How you play

The players are shown the object that is going to be hidden. One player is chosen and sent out of the room. The other players agree a hiding place for the object and hide it. It can be hidden anywhere or on anyone in the room. The player who was sent outside is called back in and begins to search. As he or she searches, everyone else sings 'How green you are, how green you are' to the first part of the tune of 'Auld Lang Syne'. As the searcher gets closer to the object the singing gets louder; if he or she starts to move away from the object, the singing gets softer.

Aim of the game

To find the hidden object by following the clues provided by the singing

Vital rules

The object should be visible but not in too obvious a place. This will depend on the sophistication and age of the players

Variations

HOT AND COLD (p. 71); HUNT THE THIMBLE (p. 76)

Find the card

TYPE OF GAME: A finding and matching game
WHO CAN PLAY: Children aged 6–10
HOW MANY CAN PLAY: Any number
WHERE YOU PLAY: Indoors

What you need

Two packs of cards; a list of all the cards in a pack

How you play

Hide the cards from one pack all over the house. Give each of the children a card from the second pack and send them off to search for the matching card. When the children bring you a matching pair of cards write their name against the card on your checklist and give them another card to find. When all the cards have been found add up the scores. The player with the highest score is the winner.

Aim of the game

To find the most pairs

Find the colour

TYPE OF GAME: A parachute game
WHO CAN PLAY: Very young children
HOW MANY CAN PLAY: It depends on the size of the parachute
WHERE YOU PLAY: Outdoors, or in a large indoor space

What you need

A parachute with different coloured segments

How you play

The children stand on top of the parachute and the adults stand round the edge holding the handles. The adults make 'waves' and the children jump up and down. Everyone chants, 'Jumping high, jumping low, red is the colour that you have to show.' The parachute is then held still and the children have to stand quickly on a red segment. The game is repeated and another colour is called out. This continues with each of the different colours being called out.

Aim of the game

To jump quickly onto the right colour – this game helps young children with learning colours

Find the sock

TYPE OF GAME: A parachute game
WHO CAN PLAY: Children
HOW MANY CAN PLAY: It depends on the size of the parachute
WHERE YOU PLAY: Outdoors, or in a large indoor space

What you need

Socks!

How you play

The children (with no shoes on) stand around the parachute holding the handles. Number the children up to ten (if using a large parachute you may have to number from one to ten twice). Practise making a mushroom shape with the parachute. When the players are ready they lift the parachute to waist height and one or more numbers are called out. Children whose numbers have been called out must peel off a sock and toss it under the parachute as far as possible. The children are then asked to make a mushroom and let go of the parachute. The sockless children must run under the mushroom, put on their sock and return to the edge before the mushroom sinks.

Aim of the game

To get out from under the parachute with your sock on before it falls back to the ground

Fist guess

TYPE OF GAME: A guessing game
WHO CAN PLAY: Children and adults
HOW MANY CAN PLAY: Any number
WHERE YOU PLAY: Indoors

What you need

Some small objects, such as coins, paper clips, Smarties, etc.

How you play

Each player is given three small objects. Putting both hands behind them, they conceal any number of their objects (or none) in one fist. On the count of three they all bring forward the clenched fist containing the objects. Each player in turn has to guess the total number of objects held in all the fists. Each player's guess must be different. When all the players have made a guess, everyone opens his or her fist and the total number of objects is counted. The player who guesses correctly, or whose guess is the nearest, wins the round.

Aim of the game

To guess the total number of objects being held in people's fists

Follow my leader

> **TYPE OF GAME:** A traditional, fairly active game
> **WHO CAN PLAY:** Children
> **HOW MANY CAN PLAY:** Any number
> **WHERE YOU PLAY:** Indoors or outdoors

What you need

No resources required

How you play

A leader is chosen. The leader starts off walking or jogging, with the other players following in a line. The followers must go wherever the leader goes and copy all the actions that the leader does. The whole game can be played with a single leader. However, it is generally better if the players take turns to lead. After a set amount of time has passed, or a certain number of actions have been completed, the current leader should go to the back of the line and the next player in line become leader.

Aim of the game

To follow in the leader's footsteps and imitate his or her actions

French cricket

TYPE OF GAME: Traditional racquet and ball game
WHO CAN PLAY: Adults, and children old enough to hold a
    tennis racquet
HOW MANY CAN PLAY: Any number
WHERE YOU PLAY: Outdoors

What you need

A child's small tennis racquet and a soft ball

How you play

One player is chosen as the batter. The other players (fielders) surround
the batter, keeping about 8 metres away. A fielder starts by throwing
the ball at the batter's legs, below the knee. The batter tries to hit the
ball away with the racquet (not too hard!). The ball is fielded by the
nearest player, who then has a turn at trying to hit the batter's legs. A
batter who manages to hit the ball is allowed to turn around to face
the next bowler. A batter who misses can only turn his or her head
(and not body) towards the bowler. If a fielder hits the batter below
the knees or catches a ball the batter has hit, the batter is out and
changes places with the fielder.

Aim of the game

To bat for as long as you can, or to get the batter out

Vital rules

Fielders must not stand too close to the batter

Ghost in the graveyard

TYPE OF GAME: A Halloween game
WHO CAN PLAY: Children
HOW MANY CAN PLAY: Any number
WHERE YOU PLAY: Outdoors (it is best played in the dark)

What you need

No resources required

How you play

One player is chosen to be the 'ghost'. A home base is decided on, for example a tree or the back door. The ghost goes off to hide, while the other players stay at the base and count to 100, before going off to hunt for the ghost. When someone finds the ghost he or she shouts 'Ghost in the graveyard!' and everyone tries to run back to base without being touched by the ghost. If a player is caught, he or she becomes the new ghost. If everyone makes it back to base the ghost has to hide again.

Aim of the game

To get back to home base without being caught by the ghost

Ghosts

TYPE OF GAME: A travel word game
WHO CAN PLAY: Older children and adults
HOW MANY CAN PLAY: Up to 7 players
WHERE YOU PLAY: In the car or on the boat or train

What you need

No resources required

How you play

The first player thinks of a word of three letters and tells the other players the first letter of the word. For example, the player may think of 'cat' and tell the others 'C'. The second player follows with another letter. This player may think of 'cracker' and tell the others 'R'. The second letter must fit with the first – that is, it must be a continuation that can eventually lead to the formation of a word – but it should not complete a word. The third player adds another letter, perhaps thinking of 'crusty' and telling the others 'U'. The other players follow on in succession. The letter given must always fit with the others but never complete a word. Inevitably, a player will eventually be forced to complete a word. He or she then becomes one-third of a ghost. Completing another word makes that player two-thirds of a ghost. Completing a third word puts him or her out of the game.

Aim of the game

To keep adding to the word and avoid becoming a ghost

Giant's treasure

TYPE OF GAME: A quiet creeping-up game
WHO CAN PLAY: Children
HOW MANY CAN PLAY: Any number
WHERE YOU PLAY: Indoors

What you need

A chair; a blindfold; a bunch of keys

How you play

A player is chosen to be the giant. The giant sits on a chair in the middle of the room, blindfolded. A bunch of keys is placed under the chair. The other players stand round the edge of the room and must take it in turns to try to steal the giant's treasure (the keys) and return to their place without being heard. A thief who is heard by the giant is out of the game. A thief who steals the keys and gets away unheard becomes the next giant.

Aim of the game

To steal the giant's treasure

Grandmother's footsteps

> **TYPE OF GAME:** A fairly active traditional game
> **WHO CAN PLAY:** Children
> **HOW MANY CAN PLAY:** Any number
> **WHERE YOU PLAY:** Outdoors or indoors

What you need

No resources required

How you play

One child is chosen to be 'Grandmother'. This child stands at one end of the room with his or her back to the other players. The players stand in a row at the opposite end of the room. Grandmother then counts (slowly or quickly) up to five and turns around. While Grandmother is counting the players may take as many steps towards her as they can, but if anyone is moving when she turns around they must go back and start again. This is repeated until a player is the first to reach Grandmother. The winning player takes the place of Grandmother for the next game.

Aim of the game

To reach Grandmother without being caught

Variations

WHAT'S THE TIME, MR WOLF? (p. 187)

Green glass door

TYPE OF GAME: A guess-the-trick game
WHO CAN PLAY: Older children and adults
HOW MANY CAN PLAY: Any number
WHERE YOU PLAY: Indoors

What you need

No resources required

How you play

One player who knows the trick keeps repeating phrases that follow the same pattern until, eventually, other players see how it is done and join in. The trick is that, as in the title of the game, the approved words contain a double letter, whereas the rejected words do not. The player begins by saying: 'Behind the green glass door you can have . . .'

He or she then continues with an approved word and a rejected word, for example: 'Shampoo – but no soap'; 'A sweet – but no chocolate'; 'A mummy – but no baby'; 'Grass – but no flowers'; 'Beef – but no pork'; 'Mutton – but no lamb'; 'Butter – but no bread'; 'Pudding – but no pie'; and so on until the other players guess the trick.

Aim of the game

To keep the game going until all of the players have guessed the trick

Guess how many

TYPE OF GAME: A quiet guessing game
WHO CAN PLAY: Children and adults
HOW MANY CAN PLAY: Any number
WHERE YOU PLAY: Indoors

What you need

Paper and a pencil for each player; a number of collections of small objects (such as a jar of sweets, a box of buttons, a bundle of pencils, a box of matches, a pin cushion with pins, etc.)

How you play

Each collection should be lettered. The collections should be placed on a table in a central position.

The players are handed paper and a pencil and asked to write down the letters that have been given to the collections of objects. They must then walk around the table, and with a brief glance at the items they must write down against each letter the number of items they imagine the container holds. The player with the nearest guess for each wins a point. Points are added up to find a winner.

Aim of the game

To guess the number of objects in each collection

Variations

HOW MANY BEANS? (p. 73)

Hangman

TYPE OF GAME: A traditional word game
WHO CAN PLAY: Children and adults
HOW MANY CAN PLAY: Usually 2 players
WHERE YOU PLAY: Indoors

What you need

Paper and a pen or pencil

How you play

At the top of the paper each player writes the letters of the alphabet. One player thinks of a word or phrase and puts a dash on his or her paper to signify each letter, for example 'party game' would be _ _ _ _ _ _ _ _ _ . The other player then asks if the word contains a particular letter. If this letter occurs in the word or phrase, the first player writes it above the corresponding dash (or dashes), and crosses the letter off the alphabet list at the top of the page. The game continues with other players guessing different letters at random and the first player filling in the letters that are guessed correctly. Every time a player guesses a letter wrongly, a line is drawn to help construct the gallows and stick figure hanging from it. The word or phrase can be guessed at any time, but if the drawing is completed before the word has been guessed correctly the first player has won the game. Players take turns at choosing and guessing.

Aim of the game

To guess the word correctly before the drawing is completed

Vital rules

Draw an agreed design before the game begins, so that the number of lines required to draw the gallows and hanging man is known

Hat changing

TYPE OF GAME: A sitting-down game
WHO CAN PLAY: People of any age
HOW MANY CAN PLAY: It depends on how many hats you have
WHERE CAN YOU PLAY: Indoors, in a fairly large space

What you need

A collection of different hats, for example a sun hat, small bowler, trilby, bobble hat, baby's hat, sombrero, etc., which should vary in size from very large to very small; a CD player, or other music source

How you play

The players sit in a circle and each is given a hat. The hats are passed around the circle when the music plays and put on when the music stops. One hat is taken away each round, and the players leave the circle as they become 'hatless'.

Aim of the game

To be holding a hat when the music stops

Variations

MUSICAL CHAIRS (p. 105); MUSICAL ISLANDS (p. 107)

The health of Colonel Bogey

TYPE OF GAME: A traditional drinking game that can also be played with non-alcoholic beverages
WHO CAN PLAY: Children and adults
HOW MANY CAN PLAY: However many players can fit around the table
WHERE YOU PLAY: Indoors

What you need

A plastic glass for every player and enough liquid to last the game

How you play

One player must know the game in advance and be the leader. The leader goes through the routine below, demonstrating what has to be done. The next time round, the other players try to follow suit.

1. Pick up the glass in an exaggerated manner (holding it between thumb and index finger, with your little finger sticking out). Raise the glass and say 'I drink to the health of Colonel Bogey for the first time.'
2. Take a sip, then put the glass down firmly. Sit down.
3. Wipe your imaginary moustache to the right and then to the left.
4. Tap the table to the right and left of the glass.
5. Tap under the table with first your right hand and then your left.
6. Stamp on the floor with first your right foot and then your left.
7. Go to stand up, then sit down suddenly.

As soon as everybody is sitting, the game begins again. Only this time Colonel Bogey's health is drunk for the second time: two sips are taken from the glass, the moustache is wiped twice, the table is tapped twice, etc. Drinking his health for the third time entails doing every action three times. On the fourth time round, the leader says 'I drink to Colonel Bogey for the last time.' This last time all the actions should be done four times and very quickly.

Aim of the game

To go through the sequence of actions in the correct order – or to get everyone in a total muddle and helpless with laughter

Vital rules

No alcohol should be used if children are playing

Heart hunt

TYPE OF GAME: An individual collecting game, especially suitable for Valentine's Day
WHO CAN PLAY: Children and adults
HOW MANY CAN PLAY: Any number
WHERE YOU PLAY: Indoors

What you need

Hearts of all shapes and sizes cut out of red, white, blue, yellow and green paper (the number needed will depend on how many players there are)

How you play

Cut each heart into four pieces. Scatter the pieces all over the room – on the floor, chairs, tables, behind the pictures, etc. Allow a set amount of time for players to collect as many pieces as they can. Then ask each player to put his or her pieces together and count how many whole hearts of the same colour have been collected.

Aim of the game

To collect as many complete hearts as possible

Vital rules

White hearts score 1 point; blue hearts – 2; yellow – 3; green – 4; and red – 5

Hearts

TYPE OF GAME: A card game
WHO CAN PLAY: Older children and adults
HOW MANY CAN PLAY: 3–7 players, though the best number is 4
WHERE YOU PLAY: Indoors

What you need

A pack of cards; paper and a pen or pencil to keep score

How you play

You win this game by having a lower score than any of the other players. The cards that you try to avoid are the hearts and the queen of spades.

All the cards are dealt. When there are 4 players, each player receives 13 cards. (See Variations for how to play with more or less than four.) The players look at the cards they have been given and select three to be given to another player (except in every fourth round – see below). Since the aim of this game is to finish with the lowest score, players tend to pass on any cards they have been dealt that score high. In this game that means the queen of spades (which scores 13) or any heart (hearts, whatever their face value, score 1 point each). Players also pass on high-value cards (the ace, king, queen and jack) from other suits, which could 'win' tricks that include the queen of spades or a heart.

When four people are playing, in the first round you pass three cards to the player on your left. In the second round, you pass three cards to the person on your right. In the third, you pass three cards to the person opposite you. In the fourth round, you have to keep all the cards that you have been dealt, and you do not pass any on. From the fifth round onwards, the same order continues: three to the left; three to the right; three to the player opposite; no passing.

The player who has the two of clubs in his or her hand always begins the game. He or she lays the two of clubs down in the middle of the table. All the other players must then lay down a card of the same suit (in this case a club) if they have one in their hand. If they cannot follow suit, they can throw away any other card. However, in the first round they may not throw away the queen of spades or a heart. No player, therefore, can get rid of any of their 'undesirable' cards in the first round, and the person who wins the first trick cannot lose any points.

The person who lays down the highest card in a particular round collects that trick. He or she must pick up the cards (the trick) and lay down another card to begin the next round. Again, the other players must lay down cards of the same suit as far as they are able. The game proceeds in this way until all the cards have been played. These will, of course, include all the hearts and the queen of spades. The players who were dealt those cards must try to play them in tricks that they do not win. The art of this game is to lose tricks skilfully.

At the end of each deal, the players look at the tricks that they have won and tot up the points contained in the tricks (1 for each heart, 13 for the queen of spades). These are recorded on the score sheet. If, for instance, the tricks a player has won include the queen of spades and the ace, ten and three of hearts, that player scores 16 points (13 for the queen of spades, 3 for the three hearts).

Although the usual aim is to win no tricks (and thus score 0 points), there is a way that a player can keep his or her score low while piling points onto all the other players. To do this a player must win all the tricks that contain the queen of spades and all the hearts. Note carefully, the player does not have to win every single trick, but to win every single trick in which a scoring card is played. A player who succeeds in winning all the hearts and the queen of spades gets a score of 0, and all the other players must add 26 points to their scores.

Play continues round by round until the tallied points of one of the players reaches an agreed level – usually 100 points. (When there are more than four players, it may be better to set the level at, say, 50.) When a player reaches this level the game stops and the person with the lowest number of points is the winner.

Aim of the game

To score fewer points than anyone else

Vital rules

Players must follow suit if they can, even if this means, for example, winning the trick that contains the queen of spades. You cannot play the queen of spades or a heart in the first round

Variations

With three players – take out the two of diamonds and deal each player 17 cards. The sequence for passing cards is: three to the left; three to the right; no passing; and then repeat. With five players – take out the two of diamonds and the three of clubs, and deal each player ten cards. With six players – take out the two and three of diamonds and the three and four of clubs, and deal each player eight cards. With seven players – take out the two and three of diamonds and the three of clubs, and deal each player seven cards

Hide and seek

TYPE OF GAME: A traditional active game
WHO CAN PLAY: Children of any age, particularly if adults join in
HOW MANY CAN PLAY: Any number
WHERE YOU PLAY: Outdoors and/or indoors

What you need

No resources required

How you play

One player is chosen to be the seeker and stands in a corner or at a 'base', eyes covered and back turned towards the other players. The other players must run and hide while the seeker counts up to an agreed number (anything from 20 to 100), then calls out loudly 'Coming, ready or not!' The other players remain perfectly still while the seeker looks for them. When found they must return to the base. The last player to be found becomes the next seeker.

Aim of the game

To be the last person to be found

Variations

If the seeker passes by a hidden player, the hidden player can make a run to the base and shout 'One, two, three, I am free.' If the seeker touches the player before he or she reaches the base, that player must help the seeker find the others. *See also* LOOK OUT FOR THE BEAR (p. 91)

Hot and cold

TYPE OF GAME: A searching and listening game
WHO CAN PLAY: Children and adults
HOW MANY CAN PLAY: Any number
WHERE YOU PLAY: Indoors

What you need

Any reasonably small but distinctive object that you can hide

How you play

The players are shown an object that is going to be hidden. One player is sent out of the room. The other players hide the object, then call back in the player who was sent outside. As he or she searches for the object, the other players help out. As the searcher gets closer to the object, the others say 'you're getting warmer'; if he or she starts to move away from the object, the others say 'you're getting colder'. The other players vary what they say depending on how close to, or far away from, the object the searcher is. For instance, 'you're cool', 'you're getting warmer', 'you're hot', 'you're absolutely boiling', etc.

Aim of the game

To find the hidden object by following the clues

Vital rules

The object should be visible but not in too obvious a place. This will depend on the sophistication and age of the players

Variations

FIND IT (p. 51); HUNT THE THIMBLE (p. 76)

Hot potato

TYPE OF GAME: An active running and catching game
WHO CAN PLAY: Older children
HOW MANY CAN PLAY: Any number
WHERE YOU PLAY: Outdoors

What you need

A tennis ball or similar

How you play

One player starts with the ball. He or she throws it up into the air, catches it, calls the name of another player and throws it to him or her. No player is allowed to hold the ball for more than one second at a time. The ball must be thrown quickly from player to player until someone drops the 'hot potato' or holds it for too long. He or she is then out of the game.

Aim of the game

To keep the hot potato passing from player to player for as long as possible

How many beans?

> TYPE OF GAME: A fairly active seeking game
> WHO CAN PLAY: Children and adults
> HOW MANY CAN PLAY: Space will determine how many can play
> WHERE YOU PLAY: Indoors or outdoors

What you need

Dry haricot beans or similar

How you play

While all the players are out of the room, the organiser hides a number of haricot beans in all sorts of places – about ten beans for each player. He or she then calls in those taking part and gives them two minutes to find all the beans they can. The player who collects the most beans is the winner.

Aim of the game

To find as many beans as possible in the time allowed

Vital rules

The players should understand that no object is to be moved in order to discover the beans. This prevents the room from being turned upside down

Variations

Smarties can be used instead of beans. *See also* EASTER EGG HUNT (p. 47); ONE FOR TEN (p. 115)

How many flies?

TYPE OF GAME: A guess-the-trick game
WHO CAN PLAY: Children and adults
HOW MANY CAN PLAY: Any number
WHERE YOU PLAY: Indoors or outdoors

What you need

No resources required

How you play

The organiser, who knows the trick, announces that he or she is holding a certain number of flies in a jar. The 'jar' is the organiser's hands, which are cupped together. The other players are told they have to guess how many flies are in the jar and that they will be given a clue. He or she will shake the jar to make the flies buzz. The organiser then shakes his or her cupped hands a certain number of times and does some buzzing, then asks a question such as 'How many flies are in the jar?'

This question is the vital clue. The number of words in the question is the number of flies in the jar. For example, if the question was 'How many flies are in this jar?' then the answer would be seven. If it was 'There are how many flies in this jar?' then it would be eight.

'How many flies?' would be three, and so on. Most players will probably assume that the number of shakes is the clue to the number of flies. They will be mistaken. It may help for the organiser to have an assistant who is in the know and can give a correct answer.

Aim of the game

To keep the other players mystified for as long as possible while they try to guess the trick

Hunt the slipper

> **TYPE OF GAME:** A traditional sitting-down game that is fairly quiet
> **WHO CAN PLAY:** Children
> **HOW MANY CAN PLAY:** Any number
> **WHERE YOU PLAY:** Indoors

What you need

A slipper

How you play

All the players except one sit close together on the floor in a circle with their knees up. The player left out (the 'hunter') brings the slipper and hands it to one of the players in the circle, saying 'Cobbler, cobbler, mend my shoe. Get it done by half-past two.' The hunter then goes away and counts to ten without looking. The object of the game is to hide the slipper from the hunter for as long as possible, so the slipper is passed rapidly around the circle under the players' knees. The hunter comes back to the circle and tries to find the slipper, while the other players continue to pass it around (trying to hide it from the hunter). He or she can challenge any player who seems to be holding it by asking 'Is it done yet?' If that player does not have the slipper, he or she says 'I think my neighbour has it.' The hunter then has to ask someone else and so the game goes on. If the game is taking too long the slipper may be tossed across the circle as well as passed around, so it is easier to follow. When the hunter correctly challenges the player holding the slipper, the two change places.

Aim of the game

To hide the slipper from the hunter for as long as possible

Vital rules

Players must own up to having the slipper if asked. Players in the circle should pretend to be passing the slipper even when someone else has it, to confuse the hunter

Hunt the thimble

TYPE OF GAME: A traditional, fairly active seeking game
WHO CAN PLAY: Children and adults
HOW MANY CAN PLAY: Any number
WHERE YOU PLAY: Indoors

What you need

A thimble

How you play

All the players but one leave the room. He or she hides the thimble in a place that is not too conspicuous, but is still in view. The others come in and hunt for the thimble. The first one who sees it sits down and remains very quiet and still until all the others have found it too. The first one who saw it then takes a turn at hiding it.

Aim of the game

To be the first to find the thimble

Vital rules

You must not give away the hiding place to the other players

Variations

FIND IT (p. 51)

Hypochondriac

TYPE OF GAME: A word and memory game
WHO CAN PLAY: Older children and adults
HOW MANY CAN PLAY: Works best with 6–8 players
WHERE YOU PLAY: Anywhere

What you need

No resources required

How you play

The first player thinks of an ailment beginning with 'A' and says, for example, 'I went to hospital because I had angina.' The second player repeats this and adds an ailment beginning with 'B', so this player might say 'I went to hospital because I had angina and bronchitis', and so on. Players drop out when they fail to remember the list correctly.

Aim of the game

To make the list of ailments as long as possible, and not to make any mistakes

Vital rules

The list must be repeated exactly

Variations

I WENT SHOPPING (p. 83)

In the air

> **TYPE OF GAME:** An active game
> **WHO CAN PLAY:** Young children aged 3 and over
> **HOW MANY CAN PLAY:** Any number
> **WHERE YOU PLAY:** In a large indoor space

What you need

A balloon (round ones are best) for each child, and some in reserve

How you play

On the word 'Go!' the children throw their balloons into the air. The child who keeps the balloon in the air the longest by batting it or tapping it wins the game.

Aim of the game

To keep your balloon in the air as long as possible

In the bag

> **TYPE OF GAME:** A quiet game
> **WHO CAN PLAY:** Children or adults
> **HOW MANY CAN PLAY:** 12 players works well
> **WHERE YOU PLAY:** Indoors

What you need

A bag for each team containing six different objects around which the players can weave a story

How you play

Players are divided into groups of four, and one of the four becomes the team leader. Each team leader is presented with a bag of objects. Each group then has five or ten minutes to prepare a story. The group that tells the funniest story, using all the objects, wins.

Aim of the game

To create an amusing story based around the objects your team is given

NOTE: A judge will be needed for the final verdict.

In the manner of the word

TYPE OF GAME: A miming game
WHO CAN PLAY: Children and adults
HOW MANY CAN PLAY: Any number
WHERE YOU PLAY: Indoors

What you need

Paper and pencils; a basket (or suitable small container)

How you play

Choose a list of adverbs and write each word on a separate slip of paper (one for each player). The slips are folded and placed in the basket. The players sit in a circle. One chooses a paper from the basket. He or she is then asked to mime performing a task, such as cleaning the car, going shopping or getting dressed, 'in the manner of the word', for example angrily, sweetly, sullenly, or hungrily. The other players have to guess the adverb. The player who guesses correctly then has a turn.

Here are some suggestions of adverbs teams could use in the game: angrily; beautifully; carefully; carelessly; cautiously; cheekily; clumsily; deliberately; delicately; disgustingly; fussily; gently; gravely; hastily; jauntily; nervously; nicely; sadly; solemnly; shiftily; silently.

Aim of the game

To guess the adverb

Variations

This can be played as a team game. The person who guesses correctly wins a point for his or her team

I pass these scissors

TYPE OF GAME: A guess-the-trick game
WHO CAN PLAY: Children old enough to hold scissors safely, and adults
HOW MANY CAN PLAY: Any number
WHERE YOU PLAY: Indoors

What you need

A pair of scissors

How you play

Two players must know the trick. One is the organiser. He or she hands a pair of closed scissors to the accomplice, who takes them and says, 'I take these scissors uncrossed and I give them crossed', opening the scissors as he or she speaks the words and moving his or her feet appropriately. The scissors are then passed to the player on the accomplice's right. That player now has to pass the scissors along, using the correct version of the formula used by the accomplice: 'I take these scissors crossed [or uncrossed] and I give them uncrossed [or crossed].' As the players go through this process, the organiser tells them whether they are right or wrong.

People who do not know the game are likely to assume that the words 'crossed' (open) and 'uncrossed' (shut) refer only to the scissors. The secret, however, is that the state of the scissors must mirror the state of the individual player's feet. If players take or give the scissors 'crossed', their feet must be crossed. If they take or give the scissors 'uncrossed', their feet should be side-by-side.

Aim of the game

To convince people that there is an unfathomable mystery to the proceedings or to work out what is going on

I remember

> TYPE OF GAME: A word travel game
> WHO CAN PLAY: Older children and adults
> HOW MANY CAN PLAY: 4–6 players
> WHERE YOU PLAY: In the car, or on a train or boat

What you need

A suitable book, magazine or newspaper

How you play

One player finds an interesting short passage to read from a book, magazine or newspaper. The other players listen carefully. The reader then asks the other players questions about the passage. The player who remembers the most things is the winner.

Aim of the game

To remember the most important points from the passage so that you can answer questions on it

Vital rules

Choose an interesting or funny passage about three or four paragraphs long

I spy

TYPE OF GAME: A traditional sitting-down game
WHO CAN PLAY: Children and adults
HOW MANY CAN PLAY: Any number
WHERE YOU PLAY: Indoors or outdoors, or in the car

What you need

No resources required

How you play

One of the players looks around and chooses an object. The player then says 'I spy with my little eye, something beginning with . . .' and states the first letter of the object chosen. The other players look around and say the name of any object they can see beginning with that letter. The first to guess correctly is the winner and chooses the next object.

Aim of the game

To work out which object the lead player has in mind

Vital rules

If very young children are playing, it is wise to say both the name and sound of the first letter of the object

I went shopping

TYPE OF GAME: A word and memory game
WHO CAN PLAY: Older children and adults
HOW MANY CAN PLAY: Works best with 6–8 players
WHERE YOU PLAY: Anywhere

What you need

No resources required

How you play

The players sit in a circle and decide who should begin. The first player says, 'I went shopping and I bought some . . .' naming a suitable item, for example, tea. The next player says 'I went shopping and I bought some tea and some sugar.' Every subsequent player repeats all the items in the list and adds another. Each player must give all the items in the correct order to remain in the game. Those who cannot, drop out. The last player in is the winner.

Aim of the game

To remember all the items, and keep them in the correct order, even when the list is very long

Vital rules

The list must be repeated exactly

Variations

There are many variations on this traditional game. Various other scenarios can be made up, for example: 'I switched on the television and I watched . . .' You can also decide that the items bought must follow in alphabetical order, and work your way through the alphabet as far as possible. The first player, for example, begins by saying 'I went shopping and I bought an apple.' The second player might then say 'I went shopping and I bought an apple and some bacon,' and so on. Anyone who forgets an article, puts them in the wrong order or cannot think of anything beginning with the appropriate letter of the alphabet must pay a forfeit (see p. 199) *See also* HYPOCHONDRIAC (p. 77)

I wrote a letter to my love

> **TYPE OF GAME:** An energetic chasing game
> **WHO CAN PLAY:** Children of any age
> **HOW MANY CAN PLAY:** Any number
> **WHERE YOU PLAY:** Outdoors, or in a large indoor space

What you need

A piece of paper, representing the letter

How you play

One child is chosen and given the letter. The other children are seated in a circle. The children sing or say this rhyme as the chosen child walks around the outside of the circle:

> 'I wrote a letter to my love
> And on the way I dropped it.
> One of you has picked it up
> And put it in your pocket.'

The chosen child then touches the backs of the others, saying, 'Not you, not you, but you'. After saying 'but you', he or she drops the letter and races off around the circle. The child behind whom the letter was dropped then runs off in the opposite direction, trying to get back to his or her place before the child who had the letter reaches it. The player who fails to get back into the ring drops the letter in the next round.

Aim of the game

To be the first to get back to the vacant place in the circle

Variations

FILLING THE GAP (p. 50); RACE ME ROUND (p. 147)

Jenkins up

> TYPE OF GAME: A team game played at the table
> WHO CAN PLAY: Older children and adults
> HOW MANY CAN PLAY: It depends on the size of the table
> WHERE YOU PLAY: Indoors

What you need

A large table; a coin

How you play

Divide everyone into two teams – A and B. The teams sit facing each other across the table. The players in Team A put their hands under the table and a small coin is passed from one to the other. When enough time has passed, Team B calls out 'Jenkins up'. The players in Team A must then hold up their closed hands. Team B then calls out 'Jenkins down', and the players in Team A must place their hands flat on the table in front of them. Team B then guess which hand the coin is under. Each person has one guess. Those on the other side must raise their hands if requested to do so. If Team B guesses correctly, the coin is handed over, they put their hands under the table and the game continues with them passing the coin and Team A guessing.

Aim of the game

To guess (or to stop the other team from guessing) where the coin is

Variations

A score may be kept, one point being given for every correct guess. The first team to reach, say, 20 points would be the winner

Jump sticks

TYPE OF GAME: An active game
WHO CAN PLAY: Children or adults (but not together because of the size issue)
HOW MANY CAN PLAY: Any number
WHERE YOU PLAY: In a large room or outdoors

What you need

Three walking sticks, canes or pieces of wood

How you play

Place the sticks on the ground parallel to each other, about 20 cm apart. Players run or walk up to the sticks and jump over them one at a time (players must keep both feet together as they jump). After each round the sticks are moved farther apart. The winner is the player who jumps the widest distance.

Aim of the game

To jump the furthest

Kim's game

What you need

A tray with between 10 and 20 objects on it. Any items can be used as long as they can all fit on the tray

How you play

The players are given two minutes to look carefully at the tray and to try to memorise the items. The tray is taken away, an item is removed and the tray is returned. The first player to correctly name the missing object is the winner and gains a point. This procedure is repeated many times and the player who has the most points at the end of the game is the winner.

Aim of the game

To use your memory and powers of observation to remember as much as you can of what is on the tray

Vital rules

The number of objects depends upon the ages of the players

Variations

Players can be provided with pencils and paper and, after they have looked at the tray for two minutes and it is removed, they write down what they have seen. (No talking!) Allow them two minutes to write, then collect the lists for checking. The most accurate list wins a small prize

Knocky, knocky

TYPE OF GAME: A family card game
WHO CAN PLAY: Children and adults
HOW MANY CAN PLAY: 4–6 players
WHERE YOU PLAY: Indoors

What you need

One pack of playing cards

How you play

Each player starts the game with five lives. The dealer deals seven cards to each player, and then everyone looks at his or her hand. The rest of the pack is placed in the centre of the table face down in a pile, and the top card is turned over and put on the table. The player to the left of the dealer now has to put down a card of the same suit as the card that is face up or a card of the same value from a different suit. In other words, if the card in the centre is the six of diamonds, the player puts down any other diamond or the six of clubs, spades or hearts. This card is placed face up on top of the first card. A player who has no suitable card to put down must take a card from the face-down pile. The top card that is face up always determines which card the next person can play.

Certain cards play a special role. If a two of any suit is placed on the pile, the player to the left has to pick up two cards, unless they can also play a two. (If the next player also puts down a two, the following player will have to pick up four!) If a jack is played, the next player misses a turn unless he or she can play another jack. If that happens, the first player without a jack misses a turn. If an eight of any suit is played, the player may change the suit being played to one of his or her choice.

When a player is left with a hand containing just one card, he or she *must* say 'Knocky, knocky. Last card.' Other players may then be able to prevent him or her from being out in the next round. A player who fails to call 'Knocky, knocky' must pick up another card on their next turn. When a player has no cards left, that round of the game is over. The remaining players add up their scores (someone must act as scorer). Any player whose cards add up to more than 21 (counting ten for all the picture cards) loses a life, two lives if they add up to more than 42, and so on. The ace of spades is the death card. A player who is left with this card immediately loses all five lives. When the scores have been added up and recorded, the game starts again and continues until only one player is left.

Aim of the game
To get rid of all the cards in your hand

Letter plates

TYPE OF GAME: A travel game
WHO CAN PLAY: Older children and adults
HOW MANY CAN PLAY: Up to 6 players
WHERE YOU PLAY: In the car

What you need
No resources required

How you play
The players are told to look carefully at the first and last letters of the number plates of passing cars. The idea is to spot the letters of the alphabet in the correct order. This is a co-operative game, so anyone can contribute the next letter.

Aim of the game

To reach the end of the alphabet by the end of the journey

Vital rules

Only the letter at the beginning or the end of the number plate counts

NOTE: Certain letters are not usually used on UK number plates, namely 'I' and 'Q', with 'Z' also being fairly rare. Allowances should be made for this.

Lie detectors

TYPE OF GAME: A sitting-down 'acting' game
WHO CAN PLAY: Older children and adults
HOW MANY CAN PLAY: Any number
WHERE YOU PLAY: Indoors

What you need

No resources required

How you play

Everyone sits in a circle and takes turns to be in the middle. The person in the middle makes three statements about him- or herself. One of these statements must be untrue. Everyone else must guess which statement is false.

Aim of the game

To detect the lie – or to pass the lie detector test

Variations

To add a competitive element to this game, the players can divide into two teams. Team members score a point for their team each time a lie goes undetected

Look out for the bear

TYPE OF GAME: An active game
WHO CAN PLAY: Young children
HOW MANY CAN PLAY: Any number
WHERE YOU PLAY: A large space, indoors or outdoors

What you need

No resources required

How you play

One child is chosen to be the 'bear' and goes off to hide while the rest, with their backs turned, stand at their base (for example, touching the wall or a fence). As soon as the children have counted to 50 or 100 they all scatter and hunt for the bear. The child who finds the bear first shouts 'Look out for the bear!' and all the children have to run back to the base. If the bear catches any of them before they reach it, they too become bears. The bears then hide together and the game continues until all the children are bears.

Aim of the game

To get back to home base before being caught by the bear

The magic stick

> **TYPE OF GAME:** A guess-the-trick game
> **WHO CAN PLAY:** Older children and adults
> **HOW MANY CAN PLAY:** Any number, but 2 must know the trick
> **WHERE YOU PLAY:** Indoors

What you need

A stick

How you play

Two players have to know in advance how the game works: the organiser and an accomplice. The organiser asks for a volunteer to go out of the room, and picks the accomplice. While the accomplice is outside, the organiser (holding the stick) decides, with the guests, on an item in the room that the 'volunteer' has to guess. All this time, the organiser is making much of the 'magic stick', saying how it can speak to certain people, how it has occult properties, etc., and generally piling on the mumbo jumbo. The time has now come for the accomplice to re-enter. From this point on the organiser uses a series of signals to indicate to the accomplice which object has been chosen. If, for example, the item chosen is a book, the organiser may call out, 'better come in now', then knock mysteriously on the floor four times, then pause and knock another four times, then say, 'knock, knock on the floor'. The accomplice, perhaps after agonising for a while, then says 'book', to the general wonderment of the others.

The key is as follows. The organiser supplies the consonants in the key word through what he or she says. Each statement begins with the relevant letter. The vowels in the key word are represented by the number of knocks on the floor: one for 'A', two for 'E', three for 'I', four for 'O', five for 'U'.

Aim of the game

To bewilder the onlookers (without getting in a muddle yourself)

Vital rules

Do not try this game if you really can't spell!

Variations

THE MOON IS ROUND (p. 100); WHAT TIME IS IT? (p. 188)

Make merry

TYPE OF GAME: A parachute game
WHO CAN PLAY: Children, especially younger children
HOW MANY CAN PLAY: It depends on the size of the parachute
WHERE YOU PLAY: Outdoors, or in a large indoor space

What you need

A parachute; a CD player or other music source and some lively music

How you play

The children hold the parachute with one hand, facing in the same direction. While the music plays the children move around in a circle. A leader calls out instructions, telling the children to walk, skip, hop, jump or run. With practice they can turn the parachute into a merry-go-round and send the colours spinning around.

Aim of the game

For the children to have fun with the parachute and to work together

Variations

When they become confident, ask the children to change direction

Memory game

> **TYPE OF GAME:** A trampoline game
> **WHO CAN PLAY:** Children
> **HOW MANY CAN PLAY:** Up to 6 players
> **WHERE YOU PLAY:** Outdoors, or in a large indoor space

What you need

A trampoline

How you play

The first player gets onto the trampoline and does a simple move. The second player does the simple move plus one other, the third player does the first two moves then adds one of his or her own, and so on. A player who forgets the sequence of moves is out of the game.

Aim of the game

To remember and perform a sequence of moves

Variations

The players could be given three lives to extend the game

Messages

TYPE OF GAME: A quiet sitting-down game
WHO CAN PLAY: Older children and adults
HOW MANY CAN PLAY: Any number
WHERE YOU PLAY: Indoors

What you need

Paper and a pencil for each player

How you play

The players write a name or word at the top of their paper. They then pass the paper to the next person, who has to write a message made up of words that begin with the letters of the word at the top of the paper – in the correct order. For example, if 'Tom Brown' is at the top of the piece of paper, the message could read: 'Today old Mrs Beckett ran over Walter's newt.' If the word is 'Jacket', the message could be: 'James and Carol kicked Eli's tortoise.' Anyone whose message is incomplete or in the wrong order has to pay a forfeit (see p. 199). Players are allowed a set amount of time to write their sentences.

Aim of the game

To write a message that makes sense (and is funny, if possible)

Miming

TYPE OF GAME: A team game
WHO CAN PLAY: Children and adults
HOW MANY CAN PLAY: Any number
WHERE YOU PLAY: Indoors

What you need

Pencils and paper; a basket (or suitable small container) for each team

How you play

The players are divided into two teams. On a small piece of paper each player writes down a word that can be mimed. (Two-part words such as 'stage fright' or 'traffic light' can be used, see p. 203 for a list of suggestions.) The players then fold their papers and place them in the other team's basket. One by one each team member chooses a piece of paper from the basket and acts out the word in mime. If the other players in their team guess the word, the team is awarded a point. Teams take turns to perform until everyone has had a turn. The scores are then added up to find the winning team.

Aim of the game

To win points by doing clever and clear mimes

Variations

The pieces of paper containing the words to be acted out can be prepared in advance. The players each take a word and sit in a circle. The players take it in turns to mime their word. As soon as the word is guessed the next player takes a turn

Mix and match

TYPE OF GAME: A finding and matching game that needs a little general knowledge.

WHO CAN PLAY: Children and adults

HOW MANY CAN PLAY: The game works best with 6–8 players

WHERE YOU PLAY: Indoors

What you need

About 30 questions written on slips of paper; the answers on another 30 slips of paper

How you play

Mix up the slips and place them on the table or floor where the players can see them. At 'Go!', the players must try to collect as many questions and matching answers as they can find within a given time, say three to five minutes.

Aim of the game

To collect more matching pairs than the other players

Vital rules

Players should be penalised for pushing or for snatching slips from other players. Perhaps a forfeit (see p. 199) would be in order, or instant disqualification. The difficulty of the questions should be adjusted according to the age of the players

Variations

CUT CARDS (p. 39)

Modern consequences

TYPE OF GAME: A pencil and paper game
WHO CAN PLAY: Older children and adults
HOW MANY CAN PLAY: It works best with about 8 players
WHERE YOU PLAY: Indoors

What you need

Paper and a pencil for each player

How you play

This is a variant of the traditional parlour game CONSEQUENCES (p. 36). It is played in the same way. Each time a player has written something down, he or she folds the paper over and passes it to the right. The scenario involves the following steps:

1. A woman called . . .
2. Who described herself (on Facebook) as . . .
3. Met a man called . . .
4. Who described himself (on Facebook) as . . .
5. They met when . . .
6. She told him he was . . .
7. He told her she was . . .
8. The consequence was . . . / They called their first baby . . .
9. And the report in OK! magazine said . . .

Aim of the game

To produce amusing scenarios

Months

TYPE OF GAME: A guess-the-trick game
WHO CAN PLAY: Older children and adults
HOW MANY CAN PLAY: Any number
WHERE YOU PLAY: Indoors

What you need

No resources required

How you play

The organiser, who knows the trick, asks one of the other players 'What month are you going away in?' That player may give any of the 12 months as an answer. The organiser then asks three further questions: a) 'What will you wear?' b) 'What will you take with you?' c) 'What will you do?' All the answers given must begin with the initial letter of the month chosen. For instance, if someone said that he or she was going away in September, 'correct' answers might be a) silk shirts, b) silver shoes and c) sail the seas. The answers will probably be mixed as the other players do not know the trick. Everyone who gives an incorrect answer pays a forfeit (see p. 199). Then the organiser questions the next player. The game continues until everyone has guessed the trick.

Aim of the game

To discover the secret and avoid paying a forfeit

Vital rules

An accomplice who also knows the trick should give some correct answers to help the other players

The moon is round

TYPE OF GAME: A guess-the-trick game
WHO CAN PLAY: Children and adults
HOW MANY CAN PLAY: Any number
WHERE YOU PLAY: Indoors

What you need

A plate

How you play

The game must be led by a player who knows the trick. That player tells the others they must do exactly as he or she does, which is to stare intently at the plate and say 'The moon is round with two eyes and a mouth', while at the same time using his or her index finger to draw an imaginary mouth and two eyes on the plate. The leader then passes the plate from his or her left hand to right hand, and then passes it to the next player, who has to repeat the actions exactly. If a player gets it wrong, he or she must pay a forfeit (see p. 199 for some suggested forfeits). The secret lies in passing the plate from your left hand to your right before passing it on to someone else, and not in the drawing on the plate. The game finishes when a player guesses the trick.

Aim of the game

To discover the trick

Variations

I PASS THESE SCISSORS (p. 80); THE MAGIC STICK (p. 92); PASSING THE WAND (p. 123)

Mr/Ms Freeze

> TYPE OF GAME: A group game
> WHO CAN PLAY: Older children and adults
> HOW MANY CAN PLAY: Any number
> WHERE YOU PLAY: Anywhere

What you need

No resources required

How you play

At the beginning of the party the organiser should announce that this game is going to be played and that when Mr/Ms Freeze freezes, everyone else must freeze too. At the same time the organiser should, on the quiet, ask one of the guests to be Mr/Ms Freeze. At some point in the party, Mr/Ms Freeze freezes. The freeze should gradually spread to the other guests as they notice. The last person to cotton on – usually because they are preoccupied with something else – becomes Mr/Ms Freeze for the next round.

Aim of the game

Not to be the last person to freeze

Murder in the dark

What you need

One playing card for each player, with one ace and one jack among them

How you play

The players choose a card, keeping their selection secret. The player who has the jack is the detective, and the player with the ace is the murderer. The detective is sent out of the room and the lights are turned off. The murderer chooses a victim and whispers 'you are dead', at which the victim screams and dies a suitably dramatic death. After the scream, the detective counts slowly to five, during which time the murderer can move closer to or further away from the victim. The detective then re-enters the room, turns on the lights and starts to question the suspects. The suspects must answer truthfully, but the murderer is allowed to lie. After a given time the detective must accuse someone. If the detective is right, the suspect confesses; if the detective is wrong, the real killer can reveal him- or herself. The cards are shuffled and the game starts again.

Aim of the game

To work out who has committed the murder

Vital rules

The detective is not allowed to ask suspects directly who the murderer is

Murder with a wink

TYPE OF GAME: A sitting-down game
WHO CAN PLAY: Any age
HOW MANY CAN PLAY: Any number, the more the merrier
WHERE YOU PLAY: Indoors

What you need

A pack of cards

How you play

Take a card for each player from the pack, one of which should be the ace of spades. Give the players a card each (only they should see it) and then collect the cards in again. The player who has been given the ace of spades is the murderer.

As the players move around the room as normal, the murderer must wink at a victim without any other player seeing. The victim waits a short while and then dies a dramatic death. The murderer must kill as many players as possible before being discovered. A player who thinks that he or she has seen the murderer winking at a victim should announce that the crime has been solved. At this point all those not dead close their eyes and the accuser touches the murderer. If the person touched is the murderer, the game ends. If not, the accuser is out of the game and the murderer seeks more victims.

Aim of the game

To solve the crime – or to get away with murder

Musical bumps

TYPE OF GAME: An active musical game
WHO CAN PLAY: Children
HOW MANY CAN PLAY: Any number (space permitting)
WHERE YOU PLAY: Indoors

What you need

A CD player or other music source

How you play

The children dance to the music. When the music stops they must 'bump' down on the floor with their legs crossed. The last child down on the floor is out.

Aim of the game

To be the last player left in

Vital rules

This game requires a sharp-eyed referee

Variations

MUSICAL CHAIRS (p. 105); MUSICAL ISLANDS (p. 107); MUSICAL STATUES (p. 109)

Musical chairs

TYPE OF GAME: An active musical game
WHO CAN PLAY: Children and adults
HOW MANY CAN PLAY: As many as you have chairs for at the
    start of the game
WHERE YOU PLAY: Indoors usually, but it can be played outside

What you need

A chair for each player; a CD player or other music source

How you play

Arrange two rows of chairs facing in opposite directions. Each player
sits on a chair. When the music begins, the players stand up and march
around the chairs while the organiser removes one chair from the rows.
When the music stops, each player tries to find a seat but someone will
now be left out. The player left standing is out of the game. The music
starts again, another chair is taken away, and the game continues. The
player who manages to sit on the last remaining chair is the winner.

Aim of the game

To be the last player left in

Variations

MUSICAL ISLANDS (p. 107)

Musical clothes

TYPE OF GAME: A dressing-up game
WHO CAN PLAY: Children and adults
HOW MANY CAN PLAY: Any number
WHERE YOU PLAY: Indoors

What you need

A bag filled with items of clothing (large knickers, funny hats, big socks, etc.); a CD player or other music source

How you play

The bag of clothes is passed around and when the music stops the person holding the bag must choose one item to wear. The game continues until all the clothes are gone from the bag. The person wearing the most items of clothing is the winner.

Aim of the game

To put on as many pieces of clothing as possible from the bag

Musical hotchpotch

TYPE OF GAME: An energetic dancing game
WHO CAN PLAY: Children, but the game can be adapted for adults
HOW MANY CAN PLAY: Any number
WHERE YOU PLAY: A large indoor area

What you need

A selection of small items – one for everyone in the game. The items chosen will depend on the age of the players and one will be a prize for the winner to keep. For children, use such things as beads, toys, an apple, a plastic beaker, etc. You also need a CD player or other music source with some lively dance music

How you play

The items are placed in the centre of the room, and all the players dance to the music. When the music stops, they each dive for an item from the pile on the floor. All the items but one are then returned to the pile and the game is repeated. This time, the player who fails to secure an item is out. The game continues until there is one item left. The player who gets the last object is allowed to keep it as a prize.

Aim of the game

To secure an item from the pile at the end of each round and win the prize

Vital rules

Someone must supervise the removal of the items round by round to make sure the correct item is left as the prize

Musical islands

TYPE OF GAME: A lively musical game
WHO CAN PLAY: Children aged 3 and up
HOW MANY CAN PLAY: It depends on the space available
WHERE YOU PLAY: In a large indoor space

What you need

Pages from old magazines (the paper needs to be of reasonably good quality); a CD player or other music source

How you play

Push back the furniture. Spread the separate sheets of paper over the floor as 'islands', leaving space all around them. When the music plays the players dance around the room, taking care not to step on the islands. When the music stops they must jump onto an empty island. A piece of paper is removed each time the music starts again and the player who does not get onto an island is out of the game. Eventually only one island remains. The player who gets onto it first is the winner.

Aim of the game

To find an island at the end of every round

Vital rules

This game needs an umpire. The first player to touch the paper wins the island, and only one player is allowed per island. No pushing!

Variations

MUSICAL CHAIRS (p. 105)

Musical lemons

> TYPE OF GAME: A sitting-down game
> WHO CAN PLAY: Children and adults
> HOW MANY CAN PLAY: As many as will fit into the space available
> WHERE YOU PLAY: Indoors or outdoors

What you need

A lemon to pass around; a CD player or other music source

How you play

The players sit in a circle and one person is given the lemon. When the music starts, the lemon is passed around the circle. When the music stops, the player who is holding the lemon drops out of the game. As the players become fewer, the game becomes faster. The game continues like this until only two players remain. The winner is the person *not* holding the lemon when the music finally stops.

Aim of the game

Not to be left holding the lemon

Vital rules

No dropping the lemon!

Variations

PASS THE PARCEL (2) (p. 127); TOSSING THE CUSHION (p. 179)

Musical statues

> TYPE OF GAME: An active musical game
> WHO CAN PLAY: Children
> HOW MANY CAN PLAY: As many as space allows
> WHERE YOU PLAY: A fairly large space. A room with furniture pushed back

What you need

A CD player or other music source

How you play

The children dance to the music. When the music stops the dancers must 'freeze' exactly as they are. The first one to move is out. The game then continues. The last person in is the winner.

Aim of the game

To survive to the end by being very still when the music stops

Vital rules

The children will need an adult to judge the game

My sister doesn't like peas

TYPE OF GAME: A guess-the-trick game
WHO CAN PLAY: Older children and adults
HOW MANY CAN PLAY: Up to 10 players
WHERE YOU PLAY: Indoors

What you need

No resources required

How you play

All the players sit in a line. The organiser sits in front of them and says to each one 'My sister doesn't like peas. What can you give her instead?' The trick of this game is that it is not the vegetable pea but the letter 'P' that 'my sister' does not like. So, if a player answers, for example, 'sweet-corn' or 'tomatoes' or 'bread,' the organiser will say, 'That's fine, that will suit her nicely.' If a player answers 'potatoes' or 'pumpkin' or 'pastry', or any other word containing a 'P', the organiser will say, 'No, that won't suit her at all', and the player will have to pay a forfeit (see p. 199). The game continues until everybody has discovered the trick.

Aim of the game

To work out the trick

Variations

'My grandmother doesn't like tea' is played in exactly the same way, but in this instance it is words that contain a 'T' that are unacceptable and bring a forfeit

Newmarket

> **TYPE OF GAME:** A family card game
> **WHO CAN PLAY:** Children and adults
> **HOW MANY CAN PLAY:** 3–8 players
> **WHERE YOU PLAY:** Indoors

What you need

Two packs of playing cards; ten counters per player

How you play

Take the ace of spades, king of hearts, queen of clubs and jack of diamonds from one pack and put aside the other cards. Place these four cards face up in the centre of the table, forming a square. Each player needs a kitty of ten counters (see p. 202 for possible alternatives). Each player must place a counter on each of the centre cards and a counter in the pool. The dealer distributes all fifty-two cards from the second pack, dealing a hand to each player, plus an extra hand. The dealer has a choice between keeping his or her own hand or swapping it for the spare hand without paying extra. If the dealer opts to keep his or her original hand, the player on the dealer's left can swap for the spare hand, but must put a counter into the pool. The spare hand can be offered round the table in this way. The player on the dealer's left then plays the first card. It can be from any suit, but must be the lowest card of that suit that he or she holds. The player places it face up on the table in front of him or her and calls out the name. The player with the next highest card in that suit calls out its name and lays it down. This continues until finally the ace is played. The player who lays down the ace then starts another sequence and lays down the lowest card of any suit that he or she holds. During the sequences a card that is the same as one of the four pay cards in the middle may be played, in which case the player who does so can pick up the counters on the matching card in the centre. Sequences are often blocked, however, because the necessary card is in the spare hand. Whenever a sequence stops, the person who played last must begin again in the same way. The counters in the pool go to the first player to get rid of all his or her cards. Any counters left on the pay cards remain for the next round.

Aim of the game

To play all your cards and win the pool

No, no and yes

> TYPE OF GAME: A talking game
> WHO CAN PLAY: Older children and adults
> HOW MANY CAN PLAY: Any number
> WHERE YOU PLAY: Indoors

What you need

A large collection of small objects to serve as counters (see p. 202 for some suggestions) – enough to give each player ten

How you play

Players are told that they cannot answer 'Yes' or 'No' to any question. If they do, they have to surrender one of their ten objects to the person who caught them out. At the end of a given time the objects are counted and the player with the most objects wins the game.

Aim of the game

To avoid answering 'Yes' or 'No' to a question

Nut race

TYPE OF GAME: A team racing game
WHO CAN PLAY: Children and adults
HOW MANY CAN PLAY: Any number
WHERE YOU PLAY: Indoors

What you need

Two bowls of large-sized nuts, such as monkey nuts

How you play

Two captains divide everyone into two teams. At each end of the room,
place a pile of mixed nuts on the floor with an empty bowl about 3 feet
from it. The teams go to opposite ends of the room and stand by their
pile of nuts. When the signal to start is given, the captains scoop up as
many nuts on the back of their left hand as they can without using their
right hand. They carry the nuts to the empty bowl at the opposite end
of the room. The team members take turns after their captain, continuing
until their pile is gone and the bowl is full. The team that fills its bowl
first is the winner.

Aim of the game

To fill your team's bowl with nuts

Vital rules

You must not use your right hand (unless you are naturally left-handed,
in which case you must not use your left hand!)

Warning

Check for nut allergies before playing this game. Some alternatives to nuts are dried chickpeas, peas or haricot beans

Off-ground touch

TYPE OF GAME: A chasing game
WHO CAN PLAY: Children
HOW MANY CAN PLAY: Any number
WHERE YOU PLAY: Outdoors

What you need

No resources required

How you play

One child is chosen to be the catcher. The other children run off, keeping within a designated area, to be pursued by the catcher. Players cannot be caught if their feet are not touching the ground. They are safe as long as they can balance on a brick, hang on a fence, etc. The catcher may wait for a player who looks likely to fall off his or her place.

Aim of the game

To avoid being caught

Variations

Only one player may take refuge above ground at any one place. Another player wishing to use the same place says 'bunk, you skunk' and the original owner then has to run somewhere else, during which time he or she is vulnerable to being caught

One for ten

TYPE OF GAME: An active outdoor game
WHO CAN PLAY: Children
HOW MANY CAN PLAY: Any number
WHERE YOU PLAY: A large space outdoors is best, such as a
    playground or garden

What you need

Packets of pipe cleaners cut into 2 cm lengths (how many depends on
how many children are playing)

How you play

Before the game starts, scatter the pieces of pipe cleaner. The children
have to find as many bits of pipe cleaner as they can, as quickly as they
can. Every time they find ten, they can trade them for one sweet. The
game organiser can continue dropping pieces of pipe cleaner around
while the game is going on. This game can continue until the sweets
run out.

Aim of the game

To collect as many pieces of pipe cleaner as possible

Vital rules

No pushing!

Variations

The number of pieces of pipe cleaner needed to trade for a sweet can
be altered

One letter more

TYPE OF GAME: A sitting-down word game
WHO CAN PLAY: Adults
HOW MANY CAN PLAY: Any number
WHERE YOU PLAY: Indoors

What you need

No resources required

How you play

The player whose first name comes first in the alphabet starts. He or she thinks of a word of three letters, announces the first letter of the word and then gives a straightforward definition of it, for example, 'The word has three letters, starts with an "A", and is a small insect' ('ant'). The player to the left must guess the word. If the guess is unsuccessful, that player is out and the game continues. A correct guess entitles the player to think of a word with four letters also beginning with 'A' and its definition, such as 'men marching to war' (army). The next player to guess correctly would need to think of and define a five-letter word beginning with 'A', then the next a word of six letters, and so on. Any player who makes a wrong guess, or cannot think of a word, drops out. The last player left is the winner.

Aim of the game

To guess correctly and construct the longest word you can

On my holiday I'll take...

TYPE OF GAME: A word game
WHO CAN PLAY: Older children and adults
HOW MANY CAN PLAY: Works best with 6–8 players
WHERE YOU PLAY: Anywhere

What you need

No resources required

How you play

The first player starts by saying 'On my holiday I'll take my . . .', and ends the sentence with any word he or she likes (the funnier the better), for instance, 'my elephant'. The next player must name an item that begins with the last letter of the previous player's item – 'T' if the first word is 'elephant'. So the next player might say 'On my holiday I'll take my trumpet.' And so on.

Aim of the game

To keep the series going

Vital rules

Players are eliminated if they do not come up with a suitable item within ten seconds

Orange race

What you need

Two large oranges

How to play

The players are divided into two teams, which must each contain an even number of players. Each team divides up into pairs. One pair from each team begins at one end of the room with an orange wedged between their foreheads. On the command 'Go!', they race to the other end of the room, touch the wall and return to the start, all without dropping their orange. If they drop the orange, they must put it back between their foreheads before they continue. When they reach the finish, they transfer the orange (by hand) to the next pair. The first team to have all its pairs complete the course wins.

Aim of the game

For all your team's pairs to get to the end of the course and back as quickly as possible

Variations

PASS THE ORANGE (p. 125)

Oranges and lemons

TYPE OF GAME: A traditional game based on an old song
WHO CAN PLAY: Mainly suitable for children aged 7 and under
HOW MANY CAN PLAY: Any number
WHERE YOU PLAY: Indoors or outdoors. Enough space is needed for the children to run around in a figure of eight and to finish with a tug of war

What you need

Someone who knows the tune and words of the rhyme. The words are as follows:

Oranges and lemons,
Say the bells of St Clement's.
You owe me five farthings,
Say the bells of St Martin's.
When will you pay me?
Say the bells of Old Bailey.
When I grow rich,
Say the bells of Shoreditch.
When will that be?
Say the bells of Stepney.
I do not know,
Says the great bell of Bow.

Here comes a candle to light you to bed.
Here comes a chopper to chop off your head!
(Chop, chop, chop, chop, chop!)

How you play

Two taller or older children are chosen. One of them is designated 'Orange', the other 'Lemon'. They stand facing each other, hold hands and raise their arms to form an arch. The other children form a line, one behind the other. Each child holds the child in front around the waist. As they sing the first 12 lines of the song, the children run under the arch, then in a circle around Orange, back under the arch, then around Lemon. The children continue to run around this circuit as Orange and Lemon chant, 'Here comes a candle ... Here comes a chopper . . .' As they chant these lines, Orange and Lemon start to move their arms up and down. On the word 'head' (or the final 'chop' if you use the extra line), Orange and Lemon bring down their arms and capture the child who happens to be passing through at that moment.

Whoever has been captured is asked in a whisper if he or she wants to be an orange or a lemon. Those who want to be oranges line up behind Orange; those who want to be lemons line up behind Lemon. The game continues in the same way until all the children have been caught. They are now in two teams facing each other, with Orange and Lemon still holding hands. The winning team is decided by a tug of war. Each team tries to pulls the other past a mark on the floor.

Aim of the game

To win the tug of war at the end of the game

Over under relay

TYPE OF GAME: A team racing game
WHO CAN PLAY: Children and adults
HOW MANY CAN PLAY: Any number
WHERE YOU PLAY: Outdoors, or in a large indoor space

What you need

Two foam footballs

How you play

The players are divided into two teams, the team members lining up one behind the other. The player at the front of the team holds the ball. On 'Go!' the first player passes the ball through his or her legs to the second player, who takes it and passes it over his or her head to the third player, who passes it to the fourth player through the legs and so on down the team. When the ball gets to the end of the line, the last person must run with it to the front of the line and the game starts again. The game ends when the player who started has returned to the front of the line; the whole team then sits down. The first team to finish and sit down is the winner.

Aim of the game

To go through the whole sequence correctly as quickly as possible

Vital rules

The ball must be passed over and under alternately

Variations

This game can be played with two round inflated balloons

Paper chase

TYPE OF GAME: A searching game
WHO CAN PLAY: Older children and adults
HOW MANY CAN PLAY: Usually up to 12 players
WHERE YOU PLAY: Indoors

What you need

Four or more identical newspapers or magazines

How you play

Players are divided into as many teams as there are papers, or play as individuals. Each player or team is given a paper. The organiser mentions a particular item, and the teams or individuals have to hunt through the paper to find it. The item can be an article, a headline, a photograph, an advertisement or, especially if playing in teams, something smaller such as a caption, a name, a phrase, or even a spelling mistake.

Aim of the game

To find the chosen item before anyone else

Vital rules

More a piece of advice: prepare this game carefully beforehand, but be flexible if necessary – allow the players to find items that fit the definition but are not the exact item that you originally found

Passing the wand

TYPE OF GAME: A guess-the-trick game
WHO CAN PLAY: Older children and adults
HOW MANY CAN PLAY: The game works best with 6–12 players
WHERE YOU PLAY: Indoors

What you need

A stick, to represent the wand

How you play

The players sit in a ring. They are told that they must do exactly what the person organising the game does. The organiser takes the wand in the right hand, transfers it to the left and passes it to the player on his or her left, saying solemnly or mysteriously: 'The wand passes.' The second player must say 'Let it pass', and take the wand. The second player then passes the wand to the third player and so on, the same words being repeated each time the wand is passed on.

The trick is simply that the wand must be taken with the right hand, passed into the left hand and then given with the left to the next player. (Nine out of ten people will pass it on without changing hands.) Those who pass the wand wrongly must pay a forfeit (see p. 199).

Aim of the game

To puzzle the players who are not in the know, until they guess the trick

Variations

I PASS THESE SCISSORS (p. 80); THE MOON IS ROUND (p. 100); SPOON PICTURES (p. 163); WHAT TIME IS IT? (p. 188)

Pass the balloon

TYPE OF GAME: A team game
WHO CAN PLAY: Children and adults
HOW MANY CAN PLAY: 2 or more teams of more than 4 players
WHERE YOU PLAY: A large indoor space

What you need

Inflated sausage-shaped balloons – enough for one per team plus plenty
of spares

How you play

Line the teams up in rows. Give a balloon to each of the team leaders,
who must place it between their knees facing forwards. On the word
'Go!' the balloon is passed down the row, from one person's knees to
the next as quickly as possible. The balloon must not be dropped or
allowed to burst, and hands may not be used. If the balloon is dropped
it must be picked up between the knees. A burst balloon is replaced by
a new one at the front of the row, and the team must start again. The
first team to pass their balloon to the last person wins.

Aim of the game

To pass the balloon along your team without dropping or bursting it

Pass the orange

TYPE OF GAME: A racing game
WHO CAN PLAY: Children or adults, but not usually together because of the height difference
HOW MANY CAN PLAY: The game works best with 10 or more players
WHERE YOU PLAY: Indoors

What you need

Two large oranges

How you play

The players are divided into two teams who form two lines. The first players in each team are given an orange which they place under their chin and hold there. On 'Go!' they must transfer the orange to under the chin of the next player, and so on. If the orange is handled or if it drops to the floor, it must be passed back to the first player in the team and the process starts again. When the last player has the orange, he or she runs or walks back to the first player and transfers it for the last time. When the first player has the orange back, he or she raises a hand. The first team leader to raise a hand is the winner.

Aim of the game

To pass the orange along your team as quickly as possible without dropping it

Variations

ORANGE RACE (p. 118)

Pass the parcel (1)

TYPE OF GAME: A sitting-down game
WHO CAN PLAY: Players of any age
HOW MANY CAN PLAY: As many as will fit into the space available
WHERE YOU PLAY: Indoors or outdoors

What you need

A gift (usually something edible, or something amusing like a large pair of knickers); large sheets of wrapping paper or newspaper; a CD player or other music source

How you play

This game needs some advance preparation. The organiser must wrap up the gift in fancy paper, then wrap up this parcel in further layers of paper (you can economise by using newspaper) until the gift is enclosed in ten or more layers. Place a sweet and/or a forfeit (see p. 199) between each layer as you go.

The parcel is passed round the circle while the music plays. The player holding the parcel when the music stops takes off a layer of paper and gets the sweet or has to do the forfeit. The music then starts again. The person who opens the final layer gets the prize.

Aim of the game

To unwrap the final layer and win the prize

Vital rules

No holding on to the parcel. The parcel must be passed along while the music plays

Variations

PASS THE PARCEL (2) (below); TOSSING THE CUSHION (p. 179)

Pass the parcel (2)

TYPE OF GAME: A sitting-down game
WHO CAN PLAY: Players of any age
HOW MANY CAN PLAY: As many as will fit into the space
available
WHERE YOU PLAY: Indoors or outdoors

What you need

Something solid to go inside the parcel; large sheets of wrapping paper or newspaper; a CD player or other music source; a prize

How you play

The organiser will have to prepare a parcel beforehand as for PASS THE PARCEL (1), however there is no need to put sweets or forfeits between layers.

The players sit in a circle. One of the players is given the parcel. When the music starts, the parcel is passed around the circle. When the music stops, the player who is holding the parcel drops out of the game. As the players become fewer the game becomes faster. The game continues until only two players remain. The winner of the game (and of the prize) is whoever is *not* holding the parcel when the music finally stops.

Aim of the game

To win the prize by being the last player left in the game

Vital rules

No dropping the parcel!

Variations

MUSICAL LEMONS (p. 108); PASS THE PARCEL (1) (p. 126)

Pass the peas please

> TYPE OF GAME: An active game that is fairly competitive
> WHO CAN PLAY: Children
> HOW MANY CAN PLAY: The game works best with 5–6 players
> WHERE YOU PLAY: Indoors or outdoors

What you need

Two plates and a drinking straw for each player; enough dried peas so that each player has six

How you play

Each player has six dried peas on his or her starting plate. Players pick up and hold a pea with their straw by sucking hard, then transfer the pea to their finishing plate. The first player to transfer all his or her peas is the winner.

Aim of the game

To transfer all your peas to your second plate

Vital rules

Peas can only be transferred using the straw

Variations

SMARTIES RACE (p. 160)

Pass the Polo

TYPE OF GAME: A quiet, sitting-down racing game
WHO CAN PLAY: Older children and adults
HOW MANY CAN PLAY: 6 or more players
WHERE YOU PLAY: Indoors

What you need

A straw for each player; some Polo mints

How you play

Two teams of equal numbers sit in rows facing each other. Everyone holds their straws with their mouths. One polo mint is slipped on to each of the two lead players' straws. On the word 'Go!' the mint is passed on to the next player's straw and so on down the team. If the mint is dropped it must be picked up using only a straw. The first team to get the mint on to the last player's straw is the winner.

Aim of the game

To pass the Polo as quickly as possible to the last player in your team

Vital rules

No hands may be used when the game is in progress

Variations

If adults are playing, the mint can be passed on cocktail sticks or toothpicks

Pass the spoon

TYPE OF GAME: A team game
WHO CAN PLAY: Usually adults
HOW MANY CAN PLAY: Any number
WHERE YOU PLAY: Indoors

What you need

Two dessertspoons attached to two very long pieces of string

How you play

Divide the players into two teams. The teams stand in a row and on the word 'Go!' they pass the spoon down inside the clothing of one team member and up inside the clothing of the next. The first team to be joined together by the string is the winner.

Aim of the game

To pass the spoon inside each team member's clothing as quickly as possible

Vital rules

If the game is played in mixed company, alternate men and women (useful but not vital!)

Pass the 2p all the way

TYPE OF GAME: A team game
WHO CAN PLAY: Children and adults
HOW MANY CAN PLAY: Enough players to make 2 teams
WHERE YOU PLAY: Indoors

What you need

A row of chairs facing each other (younger players can sit in rows cross-legged on the floor); two 2p coins

How you play

The players sit in two rows facing each other. Everybody makes both hands into fists and holds them out with the backs of their hands facing up. A 2p coin is placed on the back of the first hand of the player at the head of each row. On 'Go!', these players slide the penny from the back of one hand onto the back of the other, and then onto the closest hand of the next player, and so on down the row. If the coin falls, it must be returned to the first player to start again.

Aim of the game

To be the first team to pass the coin to the end of the row

Vital rules

Team games may need a referee to keep order

Peanut race

What you need

Two bags of peanuts; two small bowls; two knives

How you play

Place the bowls on a table at one end of the room. Place the bags of peanuts and knives at the other end of the room on another table. An organiser is needed to give the signal to start, to watch the time and to keep a tally of the peanuts.

The players choose partners to play with and each pair in turn does the following. They go to the table with the peanuts, take a knife each and, when the organiser says 'Go!', place as many peanuts as possible on the knife blade. They both then carry the knife with one hand to the other end of the room, deposit the peanuts in the bowl and return for more. They can make as many trips as time allows. Try three minutes. When the time is up, the organiser says 'Stop' and counts the total number of peanuts in the two bowls, which is the score for that pair. When every pair has had a turn, the pair that carried the most peanuts is the winner.

Aim of the game

To get more peanuts into your bowls than your opponents

Vital rules

Only one hand should be used to carry the knife. If children are playing, plastic knives should be used

Warning

Check for nut allergies before playing this game. Dried peas make the best alternative to peanuts

Pens, paper, action!

TYPE OF GAME: A drawing and guessing game
WHO CAN PLAY: Children familiar enough with the subject matter to have a realistic chance of guessing the answer, and adults
HOW MANY CAN PLAY: The game works best with 6 or more players
WHERE YOU PLAY: Indoors

What you need

Plenty of paper and pens or pencils; a list of film titles (see p. 204 for some suggestions)

How you play

Players are divided into teams. At least one organiser is needed to feed information to the teams from the list. One member from each team goes up to the person holding the list. The organiser quietly tells the team representatives the title of the first film on the list, or shows them the title, carefully concealing the rest of the list. The representatives go back to their teams and draw a sketch to represent the title, on a piece of paper. The other members of the team try to guess what the title is. When someone works out the correct answer (being careful not to let the other team overhear), that person goes back to the organiser, whispers the correct answer, and is given the name of the next film on the list. This process continues until the end of the list is reached. The first team to reach the end of the list wins.

Aim of the game

To convey film titles through drawings to the other members of the team

Vital rules

Words cannot be written down or spoken by the member of the team who is doing the drawing

Variations

The game can be played with book titles, song titles or anything that people can reasonably be expected to draw. For a similar game that is more suitable for children, *see* QUICK ON THE DRAW (p. 146)

Pick a picture

TYPE OF GAME: A seeking and designing game
WHO CAN PLAY: Young children
HOW MANY CAN PLAY: Any number
WHERE YOU PLAY: Outdoors

What you need

Small pieces of card (roughly 10 cm by 10 cm); double-sided tape

How you play

Cut enough cards for each player to have one. Cover one side of each piece of card with double-sided tape. Find an outdoor area where children can find a variety of interesting and colourful small objects safely (and without upsetting the gardener). Each child is given a card and sent outdoors to make a picture. They may choose to stick on petals, leaves, ferns, small stones, daisies, etc. They can make a picture or a pattern. A discerning adult then calls them all together and awards a prize for the best composition. (It is advisable to have small runners-up prizes for all participants.)

Aim of the game

To produce a pretty picture from the materials available

Vital rules

Make it clear to the children which flowers they can pick for their picture

Pick a popstar

TYPE OF GAME: A singing and imitating game
WHO CAN PLAY: Older children and adults
HOW MANY CAN PLAY: Any number
WHERE YOU PLAY: Indoors

What you need

Folded-up pieces of paper with the names of various well-known popstars; a dish or hat to put them in

How you play

Each of the guests picks a piece of paper from the hat. When it is that player's turn, he or she has to sing a verse of a song made famous by that particular popstar – if possible imitating the star's singing style. The other guests have to guess the name of the star, and can award points for the quality of the performance.

Aim of the game

To impress with your singing and your knowledge of pop

Pinocchio's nose

TYPE OF GAME: An energetic chasing game
WHO CAN PLAY: Children
HOW MANY CAN PLAY: Any number
WHERE YOU PLAY: Outdoors

What you need

No resources required

How you play

One child is chosen to be the chaser. When the chaser tags another player, that player joins hands with the chaser and they run together to catch a third person, who then runs with them to catch a fourth, and so on. The line gets longer and longer until only one player remains uncaught. The last player starts off a new game.

Aim of the game

To not be caught for as long as possible

Vital rules

The players at both ends of the growing 'nose' can catch those still running free

Pin the tail on the donkey

TYPE OF GAME: A traditional game

WHO CAN PLAY: It is a favourite at children's parties but can be played by anyone

HOW MANY CAN PLAY: Any number

WHERE YOU PLAY: Usually indoors

What you need

A piece of board (pinboard is best); a blindfold; a large sheet of paper with an outline of a donkey (without a tail) drawn on it (copy the drawing from a book); a drawing pin. Colour in the donkey and make a black mark where the tail should hang. Make a detached donkey's tail from anything that can be pinned to the drawing

How you play

The donkey is propped up against a wall. Taking it in turns to be blindfolded, the players are handed the tail and told they have to pin it in its correct position on the donkey. When they have had their go, the blindfold is removed and they can inspect their handiwork. The position where they placed the tail is marked with their name, and the tail itself is removed and passed to the next player. When all the players have had a turn, the pinhole nearest to the black spot is the winner.

Aim of the game

To place the donkey's tail as near as possible to its correct position

Place to place

What you need

No resources required

How you play

The first player thinks of the name of a town or city anywhere in the world and calls it out. The second player immediately tries to think of another whose first letter is the same as the last letter of the name just called. For example, the first player may say 'Bristol', the next 'London', the next 'Nantes,' and so on. No place may be used more than once.

Aim of the game

To keep the sequence going for as long as possible

Vital rules

A time limit of 15 seconds is allowed for each player to think of a name – other players may count out loud. Anyone who fails to think of a new name in time drops out

Variations

The towns or cities can be limited to the UK. This game can, of course, also be played at home

Poor Pussy

TYPE OF GAME: A sitting-down game
WHO CAN PLAY: Children and adults
HOW MANY CAN PLAY: Any number
WHERE YOU PLAY: Indoors

What you need

No resources required

How you play

All the players but one sit in a circle, the odd one out being 'Pussy'. Pussy kneels in front of a player in the circle and says, in pitiful tones, 'Meow!' The player addressed in this way must say, without smiling, 'Poor Pussy'. Pussy meows at each player three times, trying hard to make them laugh. If they do laugh, they change places with Pussy. If not, Pussy moves on to the next person in the circle.

Aim of the game

To make one of the other players laugh

Postman

TYPE OF GAME: An active game
WHO CAN PLAY: Children and adults
HOW MANY CAN PLAY: Any number
WHERE YOU PLAY: Indoors or outdoors

What you need

Small cards with names of towns or cities written on them; a blindfold

How you play

The players sit in a circle. One is chosen to be the 'postman' and is blindfolded. Another is chosen to be the 'postmaster'. He or she gives each player a card with the name of a town or city written on it, then stands outside the ring to give orders. The postman stands inside the circle. The postmaster says 'I have sent a letter from . . . to . . .', naming two of the places on the cards. The players holding these cards then have to change places. As they move across the circle the postman tries to capture one of them. If successful, the postman takes that person's place and the captured player becomes the postman. The postmaster should call out the place names fairly rapidly, and if a player remains seated when his or her card is called, he or she has to be the postman. If the postmaster says 'General delivery' all the players must change places, and the postman tries to take over any vacant place.

Aim of the game

To follow the postmaster's instructions, and to avoid being captured by the postman

Priest of the parish

> **TYPE OF GAME:** A lively memory game
> **WHO CAN PLAY:** Older children and adults
> **HOW MANY CAN PLAY:** Any number
> **WHERE YOU PLAY:** Indoors

What you need

A chair for each player

How you play

The chairs are arranged in a circle and each chair is given a number, with number 1 being nearest to the organiser who leads the game.

The organiser starts the game by saying: 'The parish priest has lost his hat. Some say this and some say that, but I say it was taken by number X.' At this point the player sitting on chair number X stands up, and he or she and the organiser have the following exchange:

> Number X: Who me, sir?
> Organiser: Yes, you, sir.
> Number X: Not me, sir.
> Organiser: Then who, sir?
> Number X: Number Y, sir.

At this point X sits down and number Y stands up and goes through the same exchange with the organiser, choosing another number at the end. Anyone who fails to stand up when their number is called or who mixes up one of the responses has to go to the highest-numbered chair and everyone else moves up a chair. This continues until the organiser decides that the players have had enough. The person who is in chair number 1 is the winner.

Aim of the game

To move up to chair number 1

Vital rules

The game should be played at a rapid pace

Variations

At large parties the game can be played by three or more teams instead of individuals. Each player needs a chair, and the chairs are organised in rows with a row for each team. The organiser accuses team X of taking the hat. All the members of team X then stand up and repeat the lines together. If a mistake is made the whole team is banished to the bottom row

Progressive pictures

TYPE OF GAME: A drawing game
WHO CAN PLAY: Children and adults
HOW MANY CAN PLAY: Any number
WHERE YOU PLAY: Indoors

What you need

Paper and a pencil for each player

How you play

The players sit in a circle, each with a piece of paper and a pencil. First, every player draws a head (animal or human), then folds the paper over to cover what has been drawn and passes it to the right. Second, every player draws a neck, shoulders and arms on the piece of paper they have received. When they fold the paper again to pass it on, they should leave two lines just visible to show the sides of the body. Third, every player completes a body. Fourth, everyone adds a skirt, trousers or legs, as the case may be. Fifth, everyone draws in a pair of feet. The papers are folded and passed on after each drawing. Finally they are all opened and passed around to be inspected and laughed over.

Aim of the game

To create amusing drawings

Pub cricket

TYPE OF GAME: A travel game
WHO CAN PLAY: Older children and adults
HOW MANY CAN PLAY: Up to 7 players
WHERE YOU PLAY: In the car

What you need

No resources required, but paper and a pencil would be useful to record the scores

How you play

Players divide into two teams. A coin is tossed to decide which team will take the first innings. The batting side scores whenever they see a pub name that includes an animal with legs. They score one run for each of the animal's legs. For example, the Swan would score two runs, the Fox and Badger would score eight, and the King William two. When a pub is passed that has no legs, such as the Ship, a wicket falls. Each side's innings goes on until ten wickets have fallen, then the other side starts to bat. The game consists of one innings for each side.

Aim of the game

To score more runs than the other team

Puss in the corner

TYPE OF GAME: An active game

WHO CAN PLAY: Children

HOW MANY CAN PLAY: 5 players

WHERE YOU PLAY: In a largish room with the furniture pushed back, or possibly in the garden

What you need

Four chairs

How you play

The four chairs are placed to form the corners of as large a square as there is room for. One player sits on each chair and one, playing the role of 'Puss', stands in the centre of the space. At the words 'Puss, puss, in the corner' the four players sitting down must leave their chairs to find another one. Puss also tries to find a seat. The player left without a seat takes the centre position and the words are spoken again.

Aim of the game

To sit on a chair and to avoid being 'Puss in the corner'

Queenie, Queenie, who's got the ball?

TYPE OF GAME: A throwing and catching game
WHO CAN PLAY: Children
HOW MANY CAN PLAY: Any number
WHERE YOU PLAY: Outdoors

What you need

A soft ball

How you play

One player is chosen to play 'Queenie' and is given the ball. Queenie stands a little way off from all the others, facing away from them. The player with the ball says 'One, two, three, throw', then throws the ball over his or her shoulder without turning around. The player who catches the ball must quickly hide it behind his or her back. When it is hidden, the players chant, 'Queenie, Queenie on the wall, who has got the golden ball?' The thrower turns around to look and then selects the player that he or she thinks has the ball. If the guess is correct the thrower has another turn. If not, the accused player swaps with the thrower.

Aim of the game

For Queenie: to guess who is hiding the ball; for the other players: to stop Queenie finding out who has the ball

Quick on the draw

What you need

Plenty of paper and pens or pencils

How you play

The players are divided into two teams. Each team produces a list of
words that they would like the other team to draw, writes each word
down on a separate small piece of paper and folds the pieces of paper
up. There should be at least as many words as there are members of
the teams. The team that is to play first selects one player to be its first
'artist'. The artist takes one of the other team's pieces of paper, unfolds
it, and looks at it without showing it to anyone. The artist then has
one minute to convey that word to his or her team members by drawing.
When the word is guessed correctly, or at the end of the minute, another
team member takes over as artist and attempts to draw another word.
Teams get a point for every word they identify before one minute is up.
When each team member has had a turn, the other team takes over.
The team that scores the most points wins the game.

Aim of the game

To convey the word through your drawing

Vital rules

The artist is not allowed to speak or to write down words

Variations

See PENS, PAPER, ACTION! (p. 133)

Race me round

TYPE OF GAME: An energetic running game
WHO CAN PLAY: Children of a similar age
HOW MANY CAN PLAY: Any number
WHERE YOU PLAY: Outdoors or in a large indoor space

What you need

No resources required

How you play

The children stand in a large spread-out circle, facing inwards with their hands behind their backs. One child is chosen to race around the outside of the circle. At some point the racer taps one of the other players on his or her hands. The tapped player then runs off in the opposite direction. The two children race around the circle in opposite directions, each trying to get back to the empty space in the circle first. The child who does not get back into the circle continues running, chooses another child's hands to tap and so on.

Aim of the game

To be the first to reach the gap left in the circle

Vital rules

To give everybody a chance to play, the children should be encouraged to tap a different player each time

Variations

CAT AND MOUSE (p. 25); I WROTE A LETTER TO MY LOVE (p. 84)

Read your rhyme

TYPE OF GAME: A sitting-down rhyming game
WHO CAN PLAY: Older children and adults
HOW MANY CAN PLAY: Any number
WHERE YOU PLAY: Indoors

What you need

Paper and a pencil for each group; a list of four fairly simple words for which it is not difficult to find rhymes (for example, 'cat', 'drain', 'hand' and 'pin')

How you play

Divide the players into pairs or teams, and give each team the four words. Teams are then required to write a rhyming poem of four lines. Each line must contain one of the given words. At least two of the lines (lines two and four) must rhyme. The rhyming word at either the end of the second or the fourth line must be one of the four words.

Aim of the game

To write the most humorous poem

Vital rules

Someone will need to be the judge. It is advisable to have other groups of words ready in case the game proves to be a hit. Other easy-to-rhyme words are: dish; fill; fit; good; green; group; light; man; name; road; sky; thing

Ring on a string

TYPE OF GAME: A calm, sitting-down game
WHO CAN PLAY: Children and adults
HOW MANY CAN PLAY: Up to 12 players
WHERE YOU PLAY: Indoors

What you need

A plain ring and a long piece of string – the length of the string will depend on the number of players

How you play

Thread the ring on to the string and tie the ends together with a knot to form a circle large enough for everyone to hold on to. All the players except one sit or stand in a circle with the string passing through their closed hands. The other player sits or stands in the middle. The players in the circle make the motions of passing the ring along the string while the player in the middle tries to find it by pointing to players in the circle. Anyone who is pointed at has to show his or her hands. As soon as the ring is found, the person who was holding it changes places with the player in the middle and the ring is passed on as before.

Aim of the game

To find out who is hiding the ring

Variations

BUTTON, BUTTON (p. 23)

Rose guess

TYPE OF GAME: A fairly quiet guessing game

WHO CAN PLAY: Mainly children, but this game is enjoyed by adults

HOW MANY CAN PLAY: Any number

WHERE YOU PLAY: Indoors

What you need

A rose; a piece of paper and a pen or pencil

How you play

Hold the rose up where everyone can see it. All the players then have to guess how many petals they think the rose has. Their guesses are then recorded on a piece of paper. The children then count the petals, and the one whose guess is nearest wins the prize.

Aim of the game

To guess the number of petals on the rose

Variations

Any flower with many petals may be used. Alternatively, a cake or something similar can be used, with everyone asked to guess the weight

Rounders

What you need

A bat and a soft ball; four markers or posts (these can be makeshift)

How you play

Set up the posts in a semicircle or square shape, leaving a good space for running between the posts (the distance will depend on the age and agility of the players!). The aim of the batters is to run around all four posts to score a rounder (or half rounder). Divide the players into two teams – A and B. Team A bats first, while Team B fields. There should be a fielder at or near each post.

Team B's bowler bowls (underarm is best) to Team A's first batter. The batter has three chances to hit the ball (after being bowled to three times the batter must run, even if he or she has missed the ball). When the ball is hit, or after a third miss, the batter drops the bat and sets off for the first post. The batter's aim is to run around as many of the posts as possible without being out. The fielders' aim is to get the batter out. There are two ways to do this. The first is to catch the ball before it hits the ground after it has been hit by the batter. The second is to touch a post with the ball when the batter is still running to reach that post (and has left the previous post).

A batter who has run to a post and sees that he or she will be out by attempting to reach the next one can stay there. Another batter takes a turn to hit, and the first batter may continue running when that other player hits the ball. There cannot be more than one batter waiting at a post at one time. A batter who runs to all four posts after a single hit scores one rounder. A batter who reaches the fourth post in stages scores a half rounder. When all the batters in Team A are out, Team B bats. The team with the most rounders wins.

Aim of the game

To score the most rounders

Sardines

TYPE OF GAME: A hiding game
WHO CAN PLAY: Children and active adults
HOW MANY CAN PLAY: Any number
WHERE YOU PLAY: All over the house, though you can declare some areas out of bounds

What you need

A reasonably large house

How you play

Switch off all the lights in the house, except in the room where all the players gather to start the game. One player is sent out and told to hide. After five minutes, the other players set out to find the missing person. Anyone who finds him or her hides in the same place as well, until there is only one player left still searching. That player then becomes the next person to hide.

Aim of the game

To get as many people as possible into a single hiding place and remain undiscovered

Vital rules

People who are hiding should keep very quiet

Variations

HIDE AND SEEK (p. 70)

Scissors, paper, stone

TYPE OF GAME: A guessing game. It can be a useful way of making decisions such as who goes first
WHO CAN PLAY: Children and adults
HOW MANY CAN PLAY: 2 players
WHERE YOU PLAY: Anywhere

What you need

No resources required

How you play

The players hide one hand behind their backs. On the count of three, they show their hand as scissors (two fingers making a horizontal 'V'), stone (fist clenched) or paper (hand held flat). The two hands are compared. Scissors beat paper because scissors cut paper, but scissors lose to stone because the stone blunts the scissors. Paper beats stone because it can wrap around stone, but it loses to scissors. Stone wins with scissors but loses with paper. If both players make the same shape with their hands, that round is a draw. The winner of the round scores a point.

Aim of the game

To try to guess what your opponent is going to do

Seat-drop wars

TYPE OF GAME: A trampoline game
WHO CAN PLAY: Children
HOW MANY CAN PLAY: 2 players at a time
WHERE YOU PLAY: Outdoors, or in a large indoor space

What you need

A trampoline

How you play

Two players face each other. They take it in turns to seat-drop (sit) and bounce, seat-drop and bounce, keeping the rhythm going. They bounce together keeping the rhythm. The first person to do it in the wrong order loses. The game can be made more difficult by altering the number of seat-drops or bounces required in the sequence.

Aim of the game

To keep the sequence of seat-drops and bounces going in the right order

Variations

Instead of seat-dropping and bouncing, the players do star jumps and bounce or a straddle jump (star jumping and touching their toes at the same time) and bounce

Sharks

TYPE OF GAME: A parachute game
WHO CAN PLAY: Children
HOW MANY CAN PLAY: It depends on the size of the parachute, but 2 players more than there are handles on the parachute
WHERE YOU PLAY: Outdoors, or in a large indoor space

What you need

A parachute

How you play

Choose two children to be the 'lifeguards' and one child to be the 'shark'. The shark goes underneath the parachute. The other children sit in a circle, pulling the parachute up to their chins by the handles with their legs underneath, making waves in the material. The shark grabs the children's legs and tries to drag them under. The two lifeguards circle the outside of the parachute ready to try to rescue children who are being pulled under by the shark. When a child is dragged under he or she becomes another shark and so on until all the children are sharks and there are no victims left.

Aim of the game

For the sharks: to capture the children sitting around the edge and turn them into sharks; for the lifeguards: to save the children from the sharks

Sight unseen

TYPE OF GAME: A quiet sitting-down game using paper and
   pencils
WHO CAN PLAY: Older children and adults
HOW MANY CAN PLAY: 10–12 people, in pairs
WHERE YOU PLAY: Indoors

What you need

A selection of common objects (such as a book, glasses case, brush,
mug, toy, etc.); pencils and paper; a chair for each player

How you play

Players form pairs and decide which of them will be the 'artist' and do
the drawing. Two chairs are placed together side by side but facing in
opposite directions. The artist takes the pencil and paper and the other
partner is given a common object. The artist must not see the object.
When the signal is given to begin, the player who has the object must
describe it without naming it. The artist must draw the object from
the description given. After a prearranged time, the pictures are collected
in and the drawing that looks most like the object is the winner.

Aim of the game

To give a clear description of the object and to make an accurate drawing
of it from the description

Vital rules

The player giving the description must not name the object he or she
is describing

Simon says

TYPE OF GAME: An active traditional game
WHO CAN PLAY: Children of any age
HOW MANY CAN PLAY: Any number
WHERE YOU PLAY: Indoors or outdoors

What you need

No resources required

How you play

One player is selected to be 'Simon'. The other players stand or sit in a circle. Simon stands in the middle and gives all sorts of orders for the children to follow. Every order given that begins with 'Simon says' must be obeyed, but if the order is not preceded by 'Simon says' the players must remain still. Any player who carries out an order not preceded by 'Simon says' must either drop out of the game or pay a forfeit (see p. 199).

Aim of the game

To obey only orders beginning with 'Simon says'

Skeletons

TYPE OF GAME: A travel game
WHO CAN PLAY: Older children and adults
HOW MANY CAN PLAY: Up to 7 players
WHERE YOU PLAY: In the car

What you need

No resources required

How you play

One player calls out the letters on a passing car's number plate. The other players take it in turns to think up words that include the letters – in the same order. For example, B-T-R could be 'better' or 'butter'. S-C-R could be 'satisfactory' or 'scenery'. Any player who fails to think of a word within one minute is out of the game.

Aim of the game

To make words out of the 'skeletons' of letters

Vital rules

Any number of letters can be added to the original three as long as those three are kept in the correct sequence

Variations

To keep all the players in the game a point system can be used. A player scores a point for a correct word but no point if he or she fails. After an agreed number of turns, the player with the highest score wins (which could be at the end of the journey). This can be a fairer way to play as some number plates (such as YYW) may prove too challenging

Sleepy zoo

TYPE OF GAME: A parachute game
WHO CAN PLAY: Very young children, with adults to help
HOW MANY CAN PLAY: It depends on the size of the parachute
WHERE YOU PLAY: Outdoors, or in a large indoor space

What you need

A parachute

How you play

The adults hold the parachute handles. The children lie down on the parachute and curl up. Everyone sings to the tune of 'Frère Jacques', but changes the words to describe a different animal each time. For example, the first time might be 'Mice are sleeping, mice are sleeping. Wake up now, wake up now. Creep about the mountains, creep about the mountains. Creep, creep, creep, creep, creep, creep.' The next time it could be frogs instead of mice, and jumping instead of creeping. The children jump up on 'Wake up now!' and the adults make the gentle waves, or 'mountains', as the children act out the words.

Aim of the game

To get children to move about in different ways

Smarties race

TYPE OF GAME: An active game that is fairly competitive
WHO CAN PLAY: Children
HOW MANY CAN PLAY: It works best with 5 or 6 players
WHERE YOU PLAY: Indoors or outdoors

What you need

Two plates for each player; enough Smarties so that each player has six;
a postcard-sized piece of card for each player, cut in half so that he or
she has two strips

How you play

Place a table at each end of the room and put a plate for each player
on both tables. Place six Smarties on each of the plates on one of the
tables. Give each player two strips of card. The players have to transfer
the Smarties, one at a time, to their plates at the other end of the
room using only the pieces of card. One card serves as a spoon for
carrying the Smartie, the other for shovelling the Smartie on to it. If a
Smartie falls to the ground, the two cards may be used to pick it up
again.

Aim of the game

To carry all your Smarties to the other end of the room using the two
pieces of card

Vital rules

Players must be able to distinguish their own plates. (Plates could be
numbered or marked with the player's initials, for example)

Variations

This game can be played with any kind of small sweets or nuts, or plastic counters such as tiddlywinks.

Sock snatch

> **TYPE OF GAME:** A chasing game
> **WHO CAN PLAY:** Older children
> **HOW MANY CAN PLAY:** Any number
> **WHERE YOU PLAY:** Indoors with a fairly big space

What you need

A pair of large socks for each player

How you play

Each player wears a pair of socks half on and half off (everyone's socks must be on to roughly the same extent). When the game starts everyone crawls around on their hands and knees trying to pull the other players' socks off. The last player with a sock left on is the winner.

Aim of the game

To keep your socks on, while trying to pull the socks off the other players

Variations

For extra excitement, this game can be played in the dark. *See also* TAIL END (p. 173)

Speeches

TYPE OF GAME: A word game
WHO CAN PLAY: Adults
HOW MANY CAN PLAY: Any number
WHERE YOU PLAY: Indoors

What you need

No resources required

How you play

One player is chosen to be the speaker and leaves the room. The other players choose a subject on which the speaker must talk for three minutes. The subject chosen may be deliberately difficult, easy or funny, depending on the personality of the speaker.

Aim of the game

To keep talking on a given subject for three minutes

Spin the plate or bottle

TYPE OF GAME: A fairly active and physical game
WHO CAN PLAY: Older children and fit adults
HOW MANY CAN PLAY: A maximum of 10 players
WHERE YOU PLAY: Indoors

What you need

A plate, bottle or other object that spins well (you will need to try this out beforehand)

How you play

The players sit in a circle. The organiser of the game gives each player a different number. The organiser spins the plate or bottle on the floor and calls out a number – say 'three'. Player number three must rush forward, grasp the plate or bottle before it stops spinning, give it another spin and, at the same time, call out another number. The player called must then rush forward to catch and spin the plate or bottle as before. A player who allows the plate or bottle to stop spinning must pay a forfeit (see p. 199).

Aim of the game

To catch the plate or bottle before it stops spinning and avoid paying a forfeit

Spoon pictures

> TYPE OF GAME: A guess-the-trick game
> WHO CAN PLAY: Older children and adults
> HOW MANY CAN PLAY: Any number, but 2 must know the trick
> WHERE YOU PLAY: Indoors

What you need

A large, shiny spoon

How you play

Two players have to know in advance how the game works; the organiser and the accomplice. The organiser asks for a volunteer to leave the room and picks the accomplice to do this. While the accomplice is outside, the organiser takes a 'picture' of one of the guests by holding the spoon up to his or her face. The accomplice is then called in and told to look at the spoon to see whose picture it is. Within a short time he or she guesses correctly, to the amazement of the guests. After many goes the guests may discover that, while the reading of the spoon is taking place, the organiser always sits in exactly the same posture as the person whose picture was taken, moving as he or she moves.

Aim of the game

To keep the players who are not in the know guessing until they work out the 'trick'

Variations

I PASS THESE SCISSORS (p. 80); WHAT TIME IS IT? (p. 188)

Spoons

TYPE OF GAME: An action game
WHO CAN PLAY: Children and adults
HOW MANY CAN PLAY: Any number
WHERE YOU PLAY: In a large indoor space

What you need

A spoon for each player

How you play

The lights are turned out, and the spoons are thrown onto the floor so that they scatter. On the signal 'Go!,' players have to pick up a spoon. The lights are then turned on. After a couple of practice rounds one spoon is removed. The game is repeated but one player will be unable to claim a spoon and is then out of the game. The game continues until only one player is left.

Aim of the game

To win the game by finding a spoon in each round

Spoony fun

TYPE OF GAME: A fairly active game
WHO CAN PLAY: Older children and adults
HOW MANY CAN PLAY: Any number
WHERE YOU PLAY: Indoors

What you need

A wooden spoon; a blindfold

How you play

All the players sit in a circle except one. This player is blindfolded and given a large wooden spoon to feel with. He or she stands in the middle of the circle, is turned around three times and advances cautiously until the spoon touches someone. Then, with the back of the spoon, the player feels that person all over. The other players must keep perfectly quiet, disguising themselves as they think fit. If the blindfolded player correctly guesses who has been touched, the two of them exchange places and the game goes on as before. If not, he or she is turned around again and has another turn.

Aim of the game

To guess the person at the other end of the spoon

Squeak, piggy, squeak

TYPE OF GAME: A fairly quiet guessing game
WHO CAN PLAY: Older children and adults
HOW MANY CAN PLAY: Works best with 6 players or more
WHERE YOU PLAY: Indoors, in a fairly big space

What you need

A blindfold; a cushion

How you play

One person is sent out of the room and blindfolded. The other players sit around the room. The blindfolded player is brought back in and given a cushion. He or she then has to find a lap to place the cushion on. When the cushion has been securely placed on a lap, the blindfolded player sits on it and says 'Squeak, piggy, squeak'. The player who is being sat on makes a squeaking sound and the blindfolded player has to guess who it is. If he or she is successful, they change places.

Aim of the game

To guess whose lap you are sitting on

Variations

BLIND MAN'S BUFF (p. 13); BLIND MAN'S STICK (p. 14)

Stepping stones

TYPE OF GAME: An active game
WHO CAN PLAY: Older children and adults
HOW MANY CAN PLAY: 4 players at a time
WHERE YOU PLAY: Indoors, in a fairly large or long space

What you need

Pages from a newspaper (preferably a broadsheet); something to mark the finishing line

How you play

Two pairs of players (traditionally a woman 'runner' is paired with a man, but any combination is possible) race against each other. The two runners stand side by side at one end of the room. Their partners each have three sheets of newspaper folded into four (in half and in half again), which they lay out on the floor. The runners have to 'race' to the other end of the room, where a rug or something similar indicates the finish. However, they must only step on the pieces of paper provided by their partner. The partner provides the stepping stones by bringing the rear paper forward as soon as it has been stepped on. A player whose foot touches the carpet is disqualified. If there are lots of players the winning couples from the first games can compete against each other.

Aim of the game

To race to the other end of the room without stepping on the carpet

Stop the bus

TYPE OF GAME: A card game
WHO CAN PLAY: Older children and adults
HOW MANY CAN PLAY: Up to 12 players
WHERE YOU PLAY: Indoors

What you need

A pack of playing cards

How you play

Play begins with one player dealing hands of three cards to each player, giving the person to his or her right an extra hand of three cards face down.

The aim in each hand is to collect three cards that are either three-of-a-kind (for example, three nines or three jacks), or three cards of the same suit that add up to 31 in total (or as close to 31 as possible). For the purposes of adding up, aces count as 11, picture cards as 10 and all other cards as their face value (a two of spades, a jack of spades and an ace of spades would amount to 23).

The player on the dealer's right examines the hand he or she has been dealt to see if it is worth keeping (i.e. whether it contains cards useful for achieving three-of-a-kind or a same-suit score close to 31). If it is a good hand, the player can choose to keep it, in which case he or she displays the contents of the spare hand in the middle of the table. If it is a poor hand, he or she displays its contents on the table and takes the spare hand without looking at it first.

Play proceeds by each player in turn exchanging either one card or all three of their cards for those displayed in the middle of the table. Once play returns to the dealer and the dealer has had a chance to make an exchange, any player is entitled to shout 'Stop the bus!' Players do this if they feel that their hand is strong enough to win, or if they realise that they cannot improve their hand by further card exchanges.

Once 'Stop the bus!' has been called, the remaining players have one more chance to improve their hands. If they do not wish to do so, they may pass, and retain the hand they have. Once all other players have either improved their hands or passed, the hands are displayed and the player with the lowest-value hand loses a life. The player on the original dealer's right now becomes the dealer.

Each player has three lives. The first player to lose all three lives has a 'dog's chance'. This allows him or her an extra life. All other players who lose all three lives go out without a dog's chance. If two players tie with the lowest score in any round, they both lose a life.

Aim of the game

To be the last player left in

Vital rules

The first player in any round may choose between the two hands but can only see one of them. Players may exchange one or three cards with those on the table, but *not* two. One round of play must be completed before a player can call 'Stop the bus!'

Stuck in the mud

> **TYPE OF GAME:** A chasing game
> **WHO CAN PLAY:** Children
> **HOW MANY CAN PLAY:** Any number
> **WHERE YOU PLAY:** Outdoors

What you need

No resources required

How you play

One player is chosen to be the 'baddie'. The other players run away and the baddie has to chase them. If the baddie manages to touch another player, that player becomes 'stuck in the mud' and has to stand still with legs wide apart. Players remain stuck in the mud until rescued by another player, who has to crawl through their legs to free them. The game continues until all the players except for the baddie are stuck in the mud.

Aim of the game

For the baddie: to get all the other players stuck. For the other players: to avoid being caught, and to release the players who are stuck

Variations

In 'Sticky toffee', players freeze when caught by the baddie. They can be unfrozen simply by a touch from another player

Suggestions

TYPE OF GAME: A word game
WHO CAN PLAY: Adults
HOW MANY CAN PLAY: 6–10 players
WHERE YOU PLAY: Indoors

What you need

No resources required

How you play

One player says a word (usually a noun), and the player sitting next to him or her follows up by saying any word suggested by the first word. This continues around the circle with each player giving a word suggested by the previous word. After a round or two the players begin to repeat the chain of suggestions backwards. Anyone who makes a slip or gets stuck loses a life, and anyone who loses two or three lives (whatever has been agreed) is dead. The last player left is the winner.

Aim of the game

To remember which words have been used by the other players and remember them in the right order

Sweet surprise

> **TYPE OF GAME:** A throwing game
> **WHO CAN PLAY:** Young children
> **HOW MANY CAN PLAY:** Up to 12 players
> **WHERE YOU PLAY:** A large space, indoors or outdoors

What you need

Three buckets containing a variety of small sweets; a tennis ball or beanbag

How you play

Mark a line on the ground or floor. Arrange the three buckets so that the first is an easy throwing distance away from that line, and the other two are further away. (The distances should be appropriate to the age of the players. You might position the first bucket approximately 1.5 metres from the line and leave approximately 0.5 metres between each bucket.) Taking it in turns to have a go, the children try to throw the ball or beanbag into the nearest bucket, then the middle bucket, then the furthest one. If they score, they take a sweet from the bucket and move on to try the next bucket. If they miss, or when they succeed with the last bucket, they pass the ball or beanbag on to the next player.

Aim of the game

To win a sweet by getting your ball or beanbag into the bucket

Swinging the apple

> **TYPE OF GAME:** A traditional Halloween game
> **WHO CAN PLAY:** Children and adults
> **HOW MANY CAN PLAY:** Works best with no more than 8
> players, who have to take turns. Part of the fun is watching
> others
> **WHERE YOU PLAY:** Indoors or outdoors

What you need

An apple with a string tied to its stalk (or you could make a small hole through an apple with a knitting needle and thread a string through the hole)

How you play

The apple is hung up by its string. Each player is allowed three attempts to bite the apple without using their hands.

Aim of the game

To eat the apple

Vital rules

Players must keep their hands clasped behind their backs

Variations

DUCKING FOR APPLES (p. 46)

Tail end

TYPE OF GAME: A chasing game
WHO CAN PLAY: Children
HOW MANY CAN PLAY: Any number
WHERE YOU PLAY: Outdoors

What you need

A whistle; a set of 'tails' for each team (these could be sports bands or socks). Each team should have a different colour set of tails

How you play

The players divide into two teams. Each team member is given a band (or sock) in their team's colour and tucks it into his or her waistband to dangle down behind like a tail. The players spread out and, when the whistle blows, they attempt to collect the tails from the opposing team. All players remain in the game even when their tails have been taken. The winning team is the first one to possess all their opponents' tails.

Aim of the game

To collect all the opposing team's tails

Vital rules

Players are not allowed to touch or hold other players in any way. The tails must be snatched by skilful running and dodging

Tangle

TYPE OF GAME: A team game
WHO CAN PLAY: Children and adults
HOW MANY CAN PLAY: 6–8 players
WHERE YOU PLAY: Indoors

What you need

A chair for each team; a ball of wool for each player (a variety of colours makes it more fun)

How you play

The players are divided into two teams and each player is given a ball of wool. Each team stands around one of the chairs. On the word 'Go!' the players weave the wool all around the chair, back, seat and legs. After an agreed time (perhaps one minute) the teams are stopped. They then swap chairs and on 'Go!' they have to untangle all the wool and wind it back up. The first team to produce neatly wound balls of wool is the winner.

Aim of the game

To create a really complicated tangle that will take the other team a long time to undo, and to untangle the other team's wool first

Vital rules

The chair cannot be lifted and the wool must not be broken

Team charades

TYPE OF GAME: A traditional miming game
WHO CAN PLAY: Older children and adults
HOW MANY CAN PLAY: Any number
WHERE YOU PLAY: Indoors

What you need

Paper and pencils

How you play

The players divide into two teams. Team A writes the title of a book, film, play or TV show on a piece of paper (see pp. 204–5 for some ideas). The members of Team A then choose a player from Team B to mime the title to his or her own team using the technique for CHARADES. If Team B guesses correctly within two minutes, it is awarded the point. Team B then chooses a member of Team A to mime a title. The game continues until all players have had a turn, and then the points are added up.

Aim of the game

To mime your title cleverly so that your team can guess it within the time limit

Tell me the word

TYPE OF GAME: A word game
WHO CAN PLAY: Adults
HOW MANY CAN PLAY: Any number
WHERE YOU PLAY: Indoors

What you need

Paper and pencils; a hat or other container

How you play

All the players write down a noun on a piece of paper and put it in the hat. The papers are then shuffled and each player picks out one. The players take it in turn to 'tell' their word to the other players, but they must never actually say it. They can choose one of three methods: explain it, act it out in mime, or draw it. The game can continue with every player writing down a verb and then an adjective.

Aim of the game

To make clear what your word is without actually saying it

Tennis ball race

TYPE OF GAME: A fairly active team game
WHO CAN PLAY: Older children and adults
HOW MANY CAN PLAY: It works best with about 12 players
WHERE YOU PLAY: A largish space is required

What you need

A chair for each player; tennis ball for each team

How you play

The players are divided into two equal teams, and the chairs are set out in two rows (facing each other) with a suitable distance between the rows. The players sit with their legs stretched out. The first player of each team is given a tennis ball, which is balanced between his or her outstretched feet. On the word 'Go!' the ball must be passed along the team from feet to feet. Players who have the ball wriggle around until their feet are over the next player's feet. They then let the ball drop gently through. If a ball drops on the floor (which it is sure to do at first) it must be returned to the beginning of the line again.

Aim of the game

To pass the ball along the row of feet to the end of your team's line as quickly as possible

Vital rules

Hands may be used only to return the dropped ball to the beginning of the line

Three lives

TYPE OF GAME: A ball game
WHO CAN PLAY: Older children
HOW MANY CAN PLAY: Any number
WHERE YOU PLAY: A large open space

What you need

A tennis ball or similar

How you play

The players all stand in a circle with their feet apart and touching the feet of their neighbours on both sides. One player bounces the ball in the middle of the circle and as soon as the ball rolls under somebody's legs that player picks it up. The rest run away. Without moving his or her feet, the player with the ball throws it at another player, trying to hit that player below the knee. After the first throw any player may pick up the ball and throw it at another, always trying to hit below the knee. Each player has three lives and may continue in the game until hit three times, at which point he or she sits out of the game. The winner is the last player left in.

Aim of the game

To avoid being hit by the ball

Vital rules

Agreed boundaries must be set before the game commences. The player with the ball must not move their feet before they throw it

Togetherness

TYPE OF GAME: A game of dexterity

WHO CAN PLAY: Children or adults

HOW MANY CAN PLAY: Any even number. This game works best when a boy is paired with a girl or a man with a woman

WHERE YOU PLAY: Indoors, the game does not require much space

What you need

A man's tie; a headscarf; a lace-up shoe; a watch

How you play

Working in pairs, players hold one of their partner's hands, and each use their free hand to attempt any or all of the following actions: tie a tie, tie a headscarf, lace up a shoe, put on a watch.

Aim of the game

To carry out an action using one hand each

Vital rules

Any pair that fails to keep holding hands is disqualified

Variations

Players in pairs try to undo a knotted handkerchief or scarf behind their backs, still using only one hand each. They must not drop the handkerchief or scarf

Tossing the cushion

TYPE OF GAME: A sitting-down game. Easy to play, but quite noisy
WHO CAN PLAY: Children and adults
HOW MANY CAN PLAY: As many as there is room for
WHERE YOU PLAY: Indoors

What you need

A small cushion; a CD player or other music source

How you play

The players sit in a circle. While the music plays they pass the cushion from person to person, the faster the better. The person holding the cushion when the music stops is out.

Aim of the game

To be the last person left in the circle

Variations

PASS THE PARCEL (1) (p. 126); PASS THE PARCEL (2) (p. 127)

Travelling alphabet

> TYPE OF GAME: A travel game
> WHO CAN PLAY: Older children
> HOW MANY CAN PLAY: Up to 6 players
> WHERE YOU PLAY: In a car

What you need

No resources required

How you play

The players try to be the first to spot things beginning with the letters of the alphabet in the right sequence, starting with 'A'. When someone spots one, he or she calls out its name, then everyone moves on to spot something beginning with 'B', and so on. Speed up the game by using initial letters from road signs or advertisements. When you come to 'X', use 'EX' instead.

Aim of the game

To spot objects whose names begin with the letters of the alphabet from 'A' to 'Z'

Variations

When travelling with younger children play the game as a 'joint' effort, the challenge being to reach the end of the alphabet

Treasure hunt

TYPE OF GAME: A traditional searching game
WHO CAN PLAY: Children and adults
HOW MANY CAN PLAY: Any number
WHERE YOU PLAY: Outdoors, or in a large indoor space

What you need

A treasure that everyone can share, such as some sweets; a pencil; paper to write clues on

How you play

Prepare the game by working backwards. Hide the treasure in an unlikely place (perhaps inside a shoe if indoors). Then write a clue that will lead to this place (in this case, '*Where my foot belongs*'). Hide this clue somewhere else, such as underneath the cat's bowl, and write a clue ('*Where the cat eats*'). Keep working backwards until you have enough clues (about 12). The final clue you write is the one you hand to the treasure seekers at the beginning of the game (they will each need a separate copy). Everyone then sets off on the trail. Players must leave the other clues in place for the treasure seekers who come after them. The first person to the treasure is the winner.

Aim of the game

To find the treasure

Vital rules

Clues should be spread out to avoid cheating

Trick the troll

> **TYPE OF GAME:** A chasing game
> **WHO CAN PLAY:** Children
> **HOW MANY CAN PLAY:** Any number
> **WHERE YOU PLAY:** Outdoors

What you need

No resources required

How you play

The 'troll' is chosen and stands on one side of an imaginary line. The other children line up opposite. The children chant: 'Please, troll, may we cross your twirling, swirling water?' The troll then chooses a colour and replies: 'Only if you're wearing . . .' Any child wearing the chosen colour has to cross to the other side without being caught by the troll. Anyone who is caught becomes the next troll.

Aim of the game

To cross to the other side of the 'twirling, swirling water' without being caught by the troll

Variations

If the children are wearing similar colours the troll can be more specific, for example, 'Only if you're wearing a blue shirt'

True or false

TYPE OF GAME: A guessing game that can be played while travelling

WHO CAN PLAY: Older children and adults

HOW MANY CAN PLAY: Up to 6 players

WHERE YOU PLAY: Anywhere, as long as there is a dictionary

What you need

A dictionary

How you play

The first player searches through the dictionary to find a word that nobody else is likely to know the meaning of. The player then has to decide whether to give the true definition of the word or to make one up. He or she states a definition confidently, and the other players have to decide whether it is true or false. If they guess correctly, the dictionary is handed on to the next player. If they are wrong, the same player takes another turn.

Aim of the game

To fool the other players with a likely sounding definition

Vital rules

The bogus definitions should sound plausible

Under the table

TYPE OF GAME: A quiet, sitting-down game

WHO CAN PLAY: Older children and adults

HOW MANY CAN PLAY: As many people as can sit around the table

WHERE YOU PLAY: Indoors

What you need

A collection of ordinary objects in a container (preferably things that have an unusual shape or texture, such as a glasses case, a walnut, a pen, a piece of fur, or a peeled grape); paper and a pencil for each player

How you play

The organiser of the game sits at the head of the table holding the basket containing the objects on his or her lap out of sight. The objects are passed one at a time from player to player underneath the table. The players have to write down the name of each object. You can add to the difficulty by waiting until all the items have been passed around before allowing the players to make their lists.

Aim of the game

To recognise the objects that are being passed around by touch alone

Vital rules

No looking!

Variations

WHAT'S IN THE BAG? (p. 186)

The vicar's cat

TYPE OF GAME: A quiet, sitting-down word game
WHO CAN PLAY: Older children and adults
HOW MANY CAN PLAY: Any number
WHERE YOU PLAY: Indoors

What you need

No resources required

How you play

One player starts by announcing. 'The vicar's cat is an admirable cat and her name is Arabella!' The next person in the circle or line continues, but moves along the alphabet, for example, 'The vicar's cat is a brazen cat and his name is Baxter', and then 'The vicar's cat is a clumsy cat and his name is Cuthbert', and so on through all the letters of the alphabet until a player fails to complete a sentence correctly. Players drop out until only the winner is left.

Aim of the game

To keep finding suitable adjectives and names beginning with each letter of the alphabet so that you are the last player left in the game

What's in the bag?

TYPE OF GAME: An easy guessing game
WHO CAN PLAY: Children and adults
HOW MANY CAN PLAY: 6–8 players
WHERE YOU PLAY: Indoors

What you need

Paper and pencils; ten familiar objects that can be recognised by touch; ten opaque plastic bags with ties, labelled one to ten

How you play

Put one object into each bag and tie up the bag. Each player will need a sheet of paper numbered one to ten down the left-hand side and a pencil. The numbered bags are then passed around one by one. After feeling carefully, each player writes down his or her guess as to what the object is against the appropriate number on the paper. When all the bags have been passed around, they are opened one by one and the contents shown. The player who has guessed the identity of the most objects correctly is the winner.

Aim of the game

To recognise the most objects by touch and feel alone

Vital rules

Papers should be passed to the left, to be marked by another player

Variations

UNDER THE TABLE (p. 184)

What's the time, Mr Wolf?

TYPE OF GAME: An active traditional game
WHO CAN PLAY: Children of any age
HOW MANY CAN PLAY: Any number
WHERE YOU PLAY: Outdoors, or in a large indoor space

What you need

No resources required

How you play

A player is chosen to be the 'wolf' and stands at one end of the room with his or her back to everyone else. The others advance towards the wolf in a row from the other end of the room, chanting 'What's the time, Mr Wolf?' The wolf spins around and says a time between 1 o'clock to 11 o'clock. When the wolf faces them, the players must freeze. Eventually, when the wolf is ready, he turns around and says: 'It's 12 o'clock, dinner time!' The children must all run back to the start without being caught by the wolf. If they are caught they either drop out of the game or join the wolf as the game is repeated, helping catch the others when the wolf calls 'Dinner time!' The game continues until everyone is caught.

Aim of the game

To avoid being caught by Mr Wolf

Variations

GRANDMOTHER'S FOOTSTEPS (p. 60)

What time is it?

TYPE OF GAME: A guess-the-trick game
WHO CAN PLAY: Older children and adults
HOW MANY CAN PLAY: Any number
WHERE YOU PLAY: Indoors

What you need

No resources required

How you play

Two players have to know in advance how the game works: the organiser and the accomplice. The organiser asks for a volunteer to go out of the room but makes sure to pick the accomplice. While the accomplice is outside, the organiser asks the rest of the players what time (what o'clock) they want the accomplice to try to guess. A time is chosen, for instance 4 o'clock. The accomplice comes in and asks the organiser 'What time is it? The organiser replies, 'Don't you know?' or 'Depends what you mean.' The accomplice then guesses 4 o'clock and everyone who is not in the know is suitably amazed. The key is that the hours from 1 to 12 are represented by the first 12 letters of the alphabet in order. Thus, 1 o'clock is represented by 'A', 2 o'clock by 'B', and so on. The organiser must be very careful to begin each answer with the letter corresponding to the chosen hour. The game continues until the secret has been discovered.

Aim of the game

To convince players not in the know that you have mysterious powers – until they guess the trick

Variations

THE MAGIC STICK (p. 92)

Wheelbarrow race

> TYPE OF GAME: A traditional children's racing game
> WHO CAN PLAY: Older children
> HOW MANY CAN PLAY: Any number
> WHERE YOU PLAY: Outdoors

What you need

A start and a finishing line

How you play

The children are divided into pairs. One member of each pair is the barrow and kneels down just behind the start line. The other member picks up the barrow's legs by the ankles, one in each hand. On 'Go!' all the pairs head off for the finishing line, the barrows walking on their hands. The first pair over the line are the winners.

Aim of the game

To be the first pair to cross the finishing line

Who am I? (1)

> TYPE OF GAME: A guessing game often played to break the ice
> WHO CAN PLAY: Older children and adults
> HOW MANY CAN PLAY: Any number
> WHERE YOU PLAY: Indoors

What you need

A card and pin for each player – each card has the name of a famous person written on it

How you play

Each player has a card pinned to his or her back so that everyone else can see it. To find out their own identity, the players ask the other guests questions about 'themselves'. Other players answer truthfully but must never reveal the actual name. The game continues until everyone has guessed the name on his or her card.

Aim of the game

To find out who you are as quickly as possible

Variations

The guests talk to each other as though they were the person whose name is on the other's back, but they do not mention the name, and from the conversation the players have to guess who they themselves are

Who am I? (2)

> TYPE OF GAME: A sitting-down guessing game
> WHO CAN PLAY: Older children and adults
> HOW MANY CAN PLAY: Any number
> WHERE YOU PLAY: Indoors

What you need

A number of sticky labels, each with the name of a famous person on it; a hat or container to put them in

How you play

A name is taken from the hat and placed on the forehead of one of the players. The player it is being stuck on must not see the name that has been taken. To discover his or her identity, the player must then ask the others questions. Once the player has guessed correctly, the next person picks a name and has a turn.

Aim of the game

To find out who you are as quickly as possible

Variations

The game can be played with the additional rule that the other players may only answer 'Yes' or 'No' to questions asked

Who is it?

TYPE OF GAME: A pencil and paper game that involves moving around

WHO CAN PLAY: Older children and adults

HOW MANY CAN PLAY: Any number

WHERE YOU PLAY: Indoors

What you need

Paper and a pencil for each player or team; a selection of photographs of celebrities and famous people taken from magazines and newspapers

How you play

Cut out the pictures, removing the names, and stick them on to card. Number the pictures and pin them up around the room. Players can work individually, in pairs or in teams. Provide players or teams with paper and a pencil and ask them to look around the room at all the photographs. They note down the number and name of anyone they recognise. After a given time, the papers are collected in and scored.

Aim of the game

To put a name to all the photographs

Vital rules

The organiser needs to keep a list of who the people are with the corresponding numbers. If people are playing in teams or pairs, they should talk to each other quietly

Who's Pig?

TYPE OF GAME: A guessing game
WHO CAN PLAY: Children and adults
HOW MANY CAN PLAY: More than 6 players
WHERE YOU PLAY: Indoors

What you need

A blindfold

How you play

One player is blindfolded. All the others sit or stand in as large a circle as possible. The blindfolded player is turned around three times, and then has to move towards the circle of players and, using only one hand, touch somebody. Once someone has been touched, the blindfolded player must keep his or her hand perfectly still and say: 'Is this Mike's pig?' The person who has been touched must reply by giving three disguised grunts. The questioner listens and if he or she is able to identify the grunter, they change places. If the grunter is identified wrongly, the blindfolded player moves on to someone else.

Aim of the game

To disguise your identity; for the blindfolded player: to guess who you are touching

Variations

BLIND MAN'S BUFF (p. 13); BLIND MAN'S STICK (p. 14); SQUEAK, PIGGY, SQUEAK (p. 166)

Wicked witches

TYPE OF GAME: An energetic and very noisy Halloween chasing game

WHO CAN PLAY: Children

HOW MANY CAN PLAY: Any number

WHERE YOU PLAY: In the garden

What you need

Two or three witches' hats

How you play

Two or three children are chosen to be 'witches' (depending on how many are playing). They put on the witches' hats and hide or huddle together somewhere in the garden. The other children skip and dance around the garden, knowing that at some point the witches will come. Suddenly the witches come screaming from the place where they have been waiting and try to catch the other players. When a witch touches someone, he or she must shout 'Freeze!' and the player who has been touched must stand still until the end of the game. The game ends when all the players have been turned to stone. The last players to be caught become the witches for the next game.

Aim of the game

To avoid being turned to stone by the witches

Variations

Witches could be monsters, dragons, or any type of beastie that suits the party you are having

Yes or no

> **TYPE OF GAME:** A sitting-down word game
> **WHO CAN PLAY:** Older children and adults
> **HOW MANY CAN PLAY:** Any number
> **WHERE YOU PLAY:** Indoors

What you need

A whistle; a gong (improvise if necessary)

How you play

Choose a referee and a question master. The referee has the gong and the whistle. Each player is questioned by the question master for one minute. While they are being questioned, players must not answer any question with the words 'Yes' or 'No' and must not nod or shake their head. The referee should time each interview and stand by with the gong, to signal when someone is out, and the whistle, to signal that someone has resisted successfully for one minute.

Aim of the game

To keep answering the questions without using 'Yes' or 'No' for as long as possible

Vital rules

The question master needs to fire questions in rapid succession

Zip and bong

TYPE OF GAME: A very simple but lively group game
WHO CAN PLAY: Older children and adults
HOW MANY CAN PLAY: Any number
WHERE YOU PLAY: Indoors or outdoors

What you need

No resources needed

How you play

The players sit in a circle. The player who begins says the word 'zip', without showing his or her teeth, to the player on his or her right. That player then says 'zip' – again with lips covering teeth – to the next player on the right, and 'zip' is passed round the circle until someone says 'bong'. Saying 'bong' has the effect of reversing the flow. The player on that player's left then either passes 'zip' to the left, or reverses the flow again by saying 'bong'. Anyone who misses their turn is out. Anyone who shows their teeth while saying 'zip' or through laughing is also out.

Aim of the game

To be the last person left in by saying 'zip' and 'bong' correctly

Vital rules

Lips must be carefully curled over teeth at all times!

Quick reference 1
Top tips and timetable for a party with games

Here are 12 handy hints for organising and running a children's party, together with a specimen timetable for a birthday party with games for children aged between four and eight.

1. If you intend to play games at the party, try not to let the number of guests get too high. About 12 is probably best. The larger the number of children, the more difficult they are to control.

2. Plan your party well in advance. Find out what resources you need for each game. Collect them beforehand and keep them in a suitable box or basket. Try out the games that you intend to play.

3. If you accept offers of adult help, which are usually very welcome, decide in advance, as far as possible, what you want your helpers to do and tell them what you have planned for them.

4. Have a game or activity in progress as the guests arrive. This means that the children can join in immediately and it gets the event off to a lively start.

5. If the party is a birthday party and presents are brought, put the presents aside and open them later. It takes a long time to open 12-plus presents, inspect them and say thank you nicely. The party may start to flag while this is going on. Do, however, make a note of who gave which present so that you can say a proper thank you eventually.

6. Alternate lively games with quiet or sitting-down games. Arrange for a quiet game to be played after the guests have eaten. Remember that older children enjoy team games more than younger ones.

7. Don't be afraid to organise the eating part of the party. If you offer a help-yourself buffet, the children are likely to heap their plates with party food and leave half of it. You are not a party pooper if you pass plates around and encourage children to eat what they have taken before they take more. It is also a good idea to pass savoury food around first and follow up with the sweet things.

8. Sometimes children won't join in the games. They should be asked to sit and watch and not be allowed to wander off. If they are simply a little shy, they will often join in when they see the other children having fun. Sometimes children cry when they take part in a game and don't win. Reassure them and tell them that everyone will get a prize at the end of the party, but don't fuss over them and do carry on with the party.

9. If you give sweets for prizes, insist that they are put aside and taken home to be eaten later.

10. If you give party bags or gifts at the end of the party, make sure that they are identical. Commercial party bags can be elaborate and expensive affairs, and yet still contain little of value. You might give each child a balloon, a cracker or party popper, a pencil and a piece of birthday cake to take home.

11. Bring the children together towards the end of the party for a joint activity. This could be listening to a story, singing songs, or copying quiet hand actions to music. This allows you to withdraw children individually as their parents arrive, and thank yous and goodbyes can then be said unflustered.

12. Try to avoid feeling that you have to compete with parties given by other parents. Children will enjoy a more modest party if it is well organised and run with a bit of imagination and a lot of good humour.

Many of these tips apply equally well to adult parties, but bring adults together at the end with coffee and brandy.

Specimen birthday party timetable

3.00 As the children arrive they join in with an adult playing 'Simon says'. Say thank you if gifts are given, but put them aside to be opened later.

3.20 MUSICAL ISLANDS

3.40 RING ON A STRING

4.00 Birthday tea with cake. Sing 'Happy birthday'. Say a general thank you for the presents before the candles are blown out. (If there are only a few guests and presents, the presents can be opened now.)

4.30 MUSICAL CLOTHES

4.50 ORANGES AND LEMONS

5.10 MUSICAL BUMPS

5.30 Get the children to sit in a circle. Play jolly music and choose one child at a time to start an action that all the others must copy. Children can be collected from the circle as their parents arrive.

Quick reference 2
Forfeits

A forfeit is a playful penalty imposed in some games on a player who makes a mistake, breaks the rules, is unable to keep the sequence going, etc. A forfeit may, for instance, be imposed in memory games such as I WENT SHOPPING when a player forgets an item or gets things in the wrong order. Sometimes forfeits are half the fun of the game – if a number of people have to do them and everyone approaches them in the right spirit. The list below contains a number of common forfeits. Hopefully, it will inspire party organisers to think of many more. Remember that it is usually best, from every point of view, to pick a forfeit appropriate to the player being penalised.

- Write your name simultaneously with two pencils. Write your first name with your left hand and your surname with your right
- Stand behind a chair and pretend to cut the hair of a difficult customer
- Pretend to hold a sheet of music and sing a song, but without making any noise
- Pretend to take a dose of nasty medicine making appropriate facial gestures
- Give a weather forecast for the following day, imitating a weather person from the television
- Sing a nursery rhyme all the way through
- Spell the first name and surname of the person on your right, backwards
- Kneel to the prettiest, bow to the wittiest, and kiss the one you love the best
- Sing in one corner of the room, sigh in another, cry in another and dance in another

- Walk round the room with an apple balanced on your head
- Work out how to put yourself through the door without opening it. (Write the word 'Yourself' on a piece of paper and push it under the door)
- Sing your national anthem standing on one leg
- Lie down on the floor, fold your arms, and get up again without unfolding them
- Read a piece of text from its reflection in the mirror
- Do a dance wearing your shoes on the wrong feet
- Imitate, without laughing, four animals named by other players
- Read three or four lines from an upside-down book
- Do the opposite of six things you are told to do
- While blindfolded, draw the face of a watch and put in the 12 numbers
- While blindfolded, tie the laces of a pair of shoes
- List, in less than one minute, ten things that can be bought in a chemist's shop
- Go round the room on one leg and one hand
- Act out selling a pair of shoes to a lady with very smelly feet
- Say five flattering things to the person on your left without using the letter 'L'
- Count backwards from 20 without making a mistake
- Tie an apron on another player at the same time as they tie an apron on you
- Be spoon-fed jelly by another player who is blindfolded
- Juggle three balls or small oranges
- Pull a face to make the person standing opposite you laugh
- Put lipstick on someone while blindfolded
- Kiss everyone at the party whose name begins with the same letter as yours
- Repeat a tongue-twister without making a mistake, for example: 'The Leith police dismisseth us' or 'Sister Susie sewing shirts for soldiers'
- Drink a glass of water from the wrong side of the glass
- Bend over backwards and kiss the wall

- Hop all around the room on one leg
- Do three press-ups
- Do a belly dance
- Get down on all fours and bark like a dog
- Do the twist
- Say something backwards, for example the days of the week or the months of the year

Quick reference 3
Counters

For games like NEWMARKET and NO, NO AND YES, any number of small objects can be used as counters. Here is a list of suggested alternatives that you might have to hand:

buttons
dried peas or beans
dried pasta shapes
cut-out candles (for a birthday party)
cut-out Christmas trees (for a Christmas party)
cut-out hearts (for a Valentine's party)
marbles
matchsticks
nuts
paper clips
pennies
penny sweets
tiddlywinks

Quick reference 4
Miming and drawing games

Some games such as MIMING and TELL ME THE WORD require teams to guess at words being drawn or acted out. Others such as CHARADES and PENS, PAPER, ACTION! involve guessing movie, book or TV programme titles. The lists below contain suggested words and titles that teams may like to use in these games.

Words

ballpoint	football	sheepdog
bedbug	gatepost	shooting star
blackbird	guard dog	sidecar
blacksmith	hairbrush	speedometer
briefcase	handwriting	spider web
broadsheet	high chair	spotlight
bus stop	keyring	stage fright
caravan	kneecap	stagecoach
catacomb	lemonade	starlight
chimney sweep	loudspeaker	sundae
cookbook	lunchtime	sunglasses
crossword	motorbike	sunshine
cupcake	motorway	sweatshirt
deadline	no one	tablecloth
door handle	paperback	teacup
earring	pigeon-toed	traffic light
eyeball	raincoat	U-turn
fast forward	sandwich	vanguard
fist fight	sausage dog	water pistol
flashlight	seaside	window pane

Titles

The African Queen (book, film)

Alice in Wonderland (book, film)

All About Eve (film)

Animal Farm (book, film)

Antiques Roadshow (TV)

Batman (film, TV)

Battlestar Galactica (TV)

Beauty and the Beast (film)

Big Brother (TV)

The Big Sleep (book, film)

The Birds (book, film)

Blackadder (TV)

Breakfast at Tiffany's (book, film)

The Bridge on the River Kwai (film)

Brokeback Mountain (book, film)

Butch Cassidy and the Sundance Kid (film)

Casablanca (film)

Casino Royale (book, film)

Charlie's Angels (film, TV)

A Clockwork Orange (book, film)

Cold Comfort Farm (book, film)

Come Dine with Me (TV)

Country File (TV)

The Crying of Lot 49 (book)

Dad's Army (TV)

A Dance to the Music of Time (book, TV)

The Deer Hunter (film)

Dial M for Murder (film)

Dirty Dancing (film)

Dr No (book)

Doctor Who (TV)

Dracula (book, film)

Duck Soup (film)

EastEnders (TV)

The Elephant Man (film)

Far from the Madding Crowd (book, film)

Fight Club (book, film)

Five Children and It (book, TV)

Four Weddings and a Funeral (film)

Frankenstein (book, film)

The Godfather (book, film)

Goldfinger (book, film)

The Good, the Bad and the Ugly (film)

Grand Designs (TV)

Grease (film)

Great Expectations (book, film)

Home & Away (TV)

The Incredibles (film)

King Kong (film)

The Land Before Time (film)

Lark Rise to Candleford (book, TV)

The Lion King (film)

The Lion, the Witch and the Wardrobe (book, film)

Little Women (book, film)

Lolita (book, film)

Lord of the Flies (book, film)

The Lord of the Rings (book, film)

The Lovely Bones (book, film)

Meet the Parents (film)

Men in Black (film)

Merlin (TV)

Monsters, Inc (film)

No Country for Old Men (book, film)

North by Northwest (film)

Notting Hill (film)

Oliver Twist (book, film)

On the Road (book)

One Flew Over the Cuckoo's Nest (book, film)

One Hundred Years of Solitude (book, film)

Pirates of the Caribbean (film)

The Pursuit of Love (book)

Pretty Woman (film)

Pride and Prejudice (book, film, TV)

The Princess Bride (book, film)

Psycho (film)

The Queen (film)

Raiders of the Lost Ark (film)

Rain Man (film)

The Reader (book, film)

Rear Window (film)

Robin Hood (TV, film)

Room on the Broom (book)

Rosemary's Baby (book, film)

The Secret Garden (book, film)

The Shell Seekers (book, TV)

The Silence of the Lambs (book, film)

Slumdog Millionaire (book, film)

The Sound of Music (film)

Spooks (TV)

Star Wars (film)

Steptoe and Son (TV)

Strictly Come Dancing (TV)

Swallows and Amazons (book, film)

The Sword in the Stone (book, film)

Taxi Driver (film)

The Thirty-nine Steps (book, film)

Three Men in a Boat (book)

The Time Traveller's Wife (book, film)

The Tin Drum (book, film)

Tinker, Tailor, Soldier, Spy (book, TV)

To Kill a Mockingbird (book, film)

To the Lighthouse (book)

Top Gear (TV)

Torchwood (TV)

Up (film)

Upstairs Downstairs (TV)

Waking the Dead (TV)

WALL-E (film)

Watership Down (book, film)

The Wicker Man (film)

Wuthering Heights (book, film)

Index

Active games

Ball games

Card games

Games for adults

Games for children or adults

Games for young children

Guess-the-trick games

Guessing games

Halloween games

Indoor games

Indoor or outdoor games

Memory games

Miming games

Outdoor games

Parachute games

Passing games

Pencil and paper games